MW01231498

My Funny Valentine

Edited By

Linton Robinson
Karla Telega

Bäuu Press
My Funny Books

CONTENTS

Married - So Very Married
By Joan Oliver Emmer

Valentine's Day kind of snuck up on me, because I'm so married. After 23 years, one doesn't need or expect the kinds of gifts or attention that we needed to nurture our relationship back in the day. It's enough for me that he doesn't ask for milk when I serve him Froot Loops for dinner. And it's enough for him that I no longer question that VERY ANNOYING HABIT of his wherein ... oh wait, Hi honey! Didn't see you sneaking up on me back there.

When two hearts beat as one ... and all that jazz.

Or maybe it's just because I don't make a fuss about ANY occasion, including, or maybe especially, birthdays. Growing up, we weren't one of those families that planned elaborate shindigs for every holiday, accomplishment or season and when we *did* celebrate, it wasn't unusual for our gift to be "wrapped" in the crumbled paper bag in which it came from the five and dime store.

So I always find myself scrambling to remember to celebrate occasions that deserve to be celebrated. For the first birthday of Thing 1, our eldest, we did what every new parent does: we rented out Madison Square Garden and booked KC and the Sunshine Band to provide the entertainment. We were also pretty excited when Thing 2's first birthday rolled around, but celebrated at home instead, with a pony and a clown who looked like Pennywise from Stephen King's *It* and scared all the toddlers into therapy.

Now, I'm lucky if I remember to grab a card and make a jello mold. By the time I realize that it's a loved one's "special day" it's often too late to order a custom cake. At that point the only cakes available are the half price ones that were never picked up by the person who ordered them and which are decorated with "*Felicitaciones* on your *Quinceañera,* Maria Teresa!!!" I once tried that on my (male) teenager and, needless to say, it took me a very long time to scrub all the pink icing off the wall and ceiling.

So don't expect a card from me on your birthday. Or a gift for your graduation. And if you're "very married" the way I am, just be glad that Valentine's Day comes but once a year...you'll only make that particular mistake once. *Feliz cumpleaños* to all.

Be Romantic or Die
By Gregg Podolski

It's Valentine's Day again, that special day when men everywhere show their love and appreciation for the women in their lives by saying: "Happy what? Oh crap! Um, I'll be right back."

When it comes to purchasing Valentine's Day gifts in a timely manner, guys generally fall into one of two categories:

1. Men who buy expensive, thoughtful gifts several days before February 14th.
2. Men who haven't recently been caught having an affair.

This is not to imply that the only men who remember Valentine's Day are philanderers. Some of them, for example, are only thinking about cheating.

As for the rest of us, it's not that we forgot to buy anything—it's just that we think it's pointless to have a special holiday dedicated to loving our women when we already worship the ground you walk on every minute of every day. Plus, we forgot to buy anything.

Don't worry, though, because we'll make up for it by also forgetting our anniversary, your birthday and, occasionally, your name. It's our little way of saying that we have no idea what we did wrong, but chances are we're going to do it again.

Besides, we know that deep down women are really just romantic sentimentalists, that material things mean little to you and all you really want for Valentine's Day is to spend some quality time with your soul mate. That, and a ring with a diamond the size of Portugal.

Making your Valentine's Day dreams come true isn't impossible, ladies. All you have to do is drop a few subtle hints in the weeks leading up to February 14th and you too can experience the singular, romantic joy of having several dozen dead flowers delivered to your office. (Suggestion: These subtle hints and reminders are most effective when your partner actually pays attention to what you're saying. The best way to ensure that this happens, we've found, is by dating women).

The first step in your quest for the perfect Valentine's Day present is to identify your significant other's price range. To do this, simply take his weekly salary, subtract the cost of living expenses, multiply the remainder by the number of weeks left until Valentine's Day, then toss that number out and go down to the nearest gas station to find out what they're charging for a dozen roses and a Snickers bar. This is what you have to work with.

Okay, so you've set your (starting) dollar amount. The next step is to mention the type of gift you're looking for in the course of casual conversation, like so:

Him: Honey, could you please pass the salt?

You: For Valentine's Day, I'd like the diamond tennis bracelet that's on sale between now and Saturday at the mall jewelry store for $599.99. Here's a picture of it, and a check that I've already filled out for the exact amount. All you have to do is sign it.

Him: Do we have any pepper?

During this step it is crucial that you resist the urge to kill him, as doing so will reduce the odds that he will remember to buy you the bracelet. (Then again, probably not by that much. Perhaps just a flesh wound would be okay).

You're almost home. Step Three is to physically drive him to the mall, walk him to the counter of the jewelry store, and have the sales clerk show him the bracelet. The hope here is that he might, at some point in the future, have a vague recollection of seeing something small and shiny. You can then build on this foundation, continuing to reference the bracelet, show him pictures of the bracelet, have his mother call and remind him about the bracelet and then, with any luck, you'll get to Step Four:

Go to the store yourself and buy the bracelet on February 15th.

I know this isn't ideally what you had in mind, but look on the bright side: You've got a new bracelet, you weren't alone on Valentine's Day, and if you put that Snickers bar in the freezer you can save it to eat with the Reese's Cup he's going to buy you on your anniversary.

A Comedy of Eros
By Barry Parham

(From pagan Rome to pajama-grams in only MM years)

Every year, in mid-February, guys do the dance. All across this great land that used to be ours, millions of American males nearly forget Valentine's Day, freak out, and then stampede the stores for flowers & candy, or power-troll the internet for prurient PJs & overdressed teddy bears.

And all because of three guys named Valentine.

How did this happen? Who *are* these three guys? And why February?

Somehow, at some point, February got this reputation as a month of romance, maybe because it's cold. Plus, football's gone and we're stuck with the wildly popular sport of bowling, where you almost *never* get to see any serious violence.

According to my exhaustive research, performed in-between today's Toyota recalls, St. Valentine's Day contains vestiges of both early Christian and ancient Roman traditions, alongside their other time-honored traditions, like hot-dish picnics and mass public executions.

> Holiday Factoid: "vestiges" is the classical Greek plural of "vest."

On this topic, the Catholic Church appears a bit confused, as they admit to recognizing at least three different Saints, all named Valentine: Valentine, Valentinus, and Val Kilmer (starring Tom Hanks as Forrus Gumpus). All three men were martyred, one of the serious downsides of achieving Sainthoodedness. Coincidence or not, they all died during various Februarys, shortly after forgetting to buy a nice gift.

One legend describes Valentine as a pagan priest who paganized around Rome during the reign of Emperor Claudius II (spelled "too") in the Third Century (spelled "III").

> Holiday Factoid: The Third Century actually went on for several hundred years, until some bright bulb finally invented "IV" (spelled "hospital feeding tube").

But on one particularly slow Ides, Claudius outlawed marriage for young men, based on his theory that single guys would be better soldiers, proving that Claudius had never met me. But Valentine continued to perform marriages in secret, until finally, on the Ides of February, around III-thirty, Claudius decreed that Valentine be - as the ancient Roman Navy Seals would put it – "martyred with extreme prejudice."

Some believe that the Christian church chose to celebrate Valentine's Feast Day in February in an effort to upstage the pagan Lupercalia festival (held on February Ides), a seriously wine-washed fertility fair dedicated to Faunus Corruptus (the Roman secretary of the Department of Agriculture), as well as to the founders of Rome, Aunt Romulus and Uncle Remus.

> Holiday Factoid: "Ides" is the classical Greek plural of "Ide."

In ancient Rome, Spring officially sprang in February, and it was a time for purification rituals (they didn't like bowling any more than we do). Houses were ritually swept clean and then, paradoxically, fouled up again by sprinkling the floors with salt and a type of wheat, paradoxically spelt "spelt." Members of the Luperci, an order of Roman priests, would then gather at the sacred cave of Rome's famous twins, Romulan and Klingon, lob some spelt around the place, and sacrifice a goat (for fertility) and a dog (for purification) and, paradoxically, they did it all with a straight face.

Afterward, young Roman boys (the Luperkinder and the Crips) would slice the goat's hide into strips, dip the strips in sacrificial blood and then hit the streets, gently slapping women with the foul things. Rather than mace-blinding the little punk truants, Roman women actually welcomed these advances, because it was believed that getting smacked with pieces of a dead goat would somehow make them more fertile, a characteristic referred to by many anthropologists as "rock stupid."

I don't even want to know what they did with the dog.

Later in the day, all these bitterly desperate young women would place their names in a big urn. The city's less-picky bachelors would then pull a name out of the urn, and the couple would be legally paired for the next CCCLXV days, or until one of them got eaten in public by lions, whichever came first.

> Holiday Factoid: I didn't have to make up anything in the previous IV paragraphs. And we wonder why aliens don't bother landing here.

Finally, around 498 AD, somebody figured out that whole "IV" thing, and the Third Century came to an end. To celebrate, Pope Gelasius ("Jelly Daddy") officially declared February XIV as St. Valentine's Day, and he hosted a huge Lupercalian "goat-strip & light hors d'oeuvres" social mixer. Sadly, the celebration soured when a Hun named Bugs Moran, who had forgotten to buy a nice gift, was massacred by Al Capone.

The first ever "valentine" greeting may have been sent by Priest Valentine himself. While serving time for running around Rome marrying people, he himself fell in love - it may have been the jailor's daughter, Nihil Corsetus, or it may have been his cellmate, Lancet Maximus. According to legend, he wrote a letter to the apple of his I, which he signed "From your Valentine," an expression that is still used today, but not in prison.

Although written Valentines were rare until after the year IV-Teen-Hundred, oral Valentine greetings were popular as far back as the Middle Ages. These feudal felicitations were usually yelled back and forth across rutted roads filled with fetid mud, Monty Python plague-carts and abandoned goat strips. Hearty knaves would hail dainty damsels, ushering in the age of the wolf whistle: "Yon Hottie! Carest thou to hie hither to my place? Truly, thou art the bomb! Fuh sooth and shizzle!"

The first commercial Valentine's Day greeting cards in the U.S. were created in the 1840s by Esther A. Howland, using lace, ribbons and colorful pictures known as "scrap," and then sold at colorful prices known as "insane."

> Holiday Factoid: "Esther A. Howland" can be rearranged to spell "Hot Snared Whale." Coincidence? I think not.

In America, over L percent of all Valentine's Day cards are purchased within II days of the day itself. One source claims that a billion Valentine cards are sent each year, while another source puts the number at 188 million, which tells me that both statistics are coming from the Congressional Budget Office.

Interestingly, 85 percent of all Valentine's Day cards are purchased by women. This is part of a sadistic, coordinated plot, hatched by the notorious FGB (Female Guilt Bombers), whose evil plan is to empty the shelves of cards, just before last call, just to spite all us last-minute losers.

And as us losers age, it gets even trickier. For every 100 single women in their 20s, there are 119 single guys, many of them unindicted. So, in that age bracket, our side can keep up with the shopping mandates. But for every 100 single women in their 60s, there are only 34 of us. Tricky. But then, thankfully, the bell curve begins to flatten: for every 100 single women over age 100, 100% of single guys are dead.

One more note - the average American consumes some 25.7 pounds of candy each year, which means that if

St. Valentine, at fighting weight, were to get dipped in chocolate, six random Americans would actually eat him.

> Holiday Factoid: There's a place in Texas called Loving County. There's also a Heart Butte in Montana, and with a name like "Heart Butte," I'm guessing they blow the bell curve on per capita candy consumption.

Ultimately, Valentine's Day, on several levels, is simply a tricky holiday for guys. Witness: I was walking through a store's Valentine's Day section when I spotted some "Nobody Else But You!" greeting cards. I thought, "What a nice confirmation of one's commitment!" And then I noticed.

The cards were sold in packs of six...

Florally Challenged
By Ernie Witham

We all felt envious of the guy with the miniature persimmon tree -- even if it had been severely pruned like that.

"Got it at OSH. Last one they had. They taped on a picture of what it's supposed to look like. See?"

"That's beautiful, man," we said, watching him head home, wishing we'd thought of the fruit angle.

The line shifted and we moved one step closer to the Happy Moments Flower Stand, which was mobbed with anxious looking guys, shuffling their feet and checking their watches. From our vantage point we could see stems, leaves and bits of ribbon flying outward as if a mower were being driven through a field. In the middle of the flurry were two frazzled young women gathering, trimming and wrapping as fast as their callused little fingers could move.

"Think they'll still have roses?" one guy asked. We looked at him like he was nuts.

Seems like just one year ago, I was in this same line with these same guys and we all swore that next Valentine's Day, we'd shop earlier.

"I completely flaked one year," the guy behind me said. "By the time I remembered, it was too late for flowers, so I grabbed two yards of sod from a landscaping job I was doing."

"Sod. Wow. Good one."

"Yeah, that's what I thought, until my wife reminded me we lived in a second-floor condo."

A relieved looking guy with glasses askew walked past us, holding a bouquet to his chest as if he were protecting a baby.

"What'd you get?"

"Something yellow."

"How long'd it take?"

"Hour and a half."

There was a groan, then one guy broke rank and ran for the five and dime. "I can't take it. I'm going with plastic petunias," he yelled.

We gave him a round of applause for bravery.

"He's dead."

"No kidding."

"How long do you think the guy that invented Valentine's Day would last if he was thrown out of a moving van into this parking lot right now?"

"Fifteen seconds, tops."

The line moved. Ahead, I could see a lot of empty white buckets that had once held cut flowers.

"I used to do jewelry," one guy said. "Bought this necklace with a little gold heart. Unfortunately, I bought exactly the same thing three years in a row. Somehow it lost its cachet."

A number of us nodded, knowingly.

Several guys left the line, then several more, then finally all of them.

"What's going on?" I asked.

"Sold out."

I approached the two young women. "You must have something!"

One of them handed me three sprigs of baby's breath and a carnation with a broken stem. "Sorry."

I lowered my head and started for my car. Then I spotted something in the back of her SUV. "What the heck is that?"

"Succulent," she said. "I'm redoing my yard at the trailer park."

I took out fifty bucks. "Can you put it into a nice pot?"

I raced home. "Happy Valentine's Day, Dear!"

Her expression said it all.

Next year, I'm going with the persimmon tree.

Happy Valentine's Day, Dear!

El Kartun

Twice a Year
By Lorraine Sears

The calendar confirmed it, there was no escape. February Fourteenth was here. Most women looked forward to Valentine's Day, or at least hoped their husband wouldn't forget. Not me, George never forgot. But then he wasn't the kind of man to buy me roses or take me out for dinner either.

When it came to a Valentine's celebration George was more practical. He thought it was the perfect date one I could never forget. So the same time every year and then six months later which, funnily enough, was around the same time as our wedding anniversary, he got his way with me. Sometimes I wondered if he planned it that way.

He came into the kitchen with that look on his face. How fast six months came round.

"Come on," he said patting my bottom, "it's only twice a year."

Easy for him to say, he wasn't the one getting poked.

Seeing my unwillingness he took my hand and with a reassuring smile, towed me reluctantly along behind him.

Ever the gentleman George made sure I was comfortable, reclining me slowly until I was staring up at the ceiling.

"Would it help if I put the radio on?" He asked, cocking an eyebrow.

I shrugged, it might, but I doubted it.

"Nothing too loud or too fast." All I needed was for him to get carried away to some pop song. He nodded and flicked on a classics station.

"Can we have the light off?" I pleaded. "It's too bright."

He frowned. "You know I can't do it without the light, June."

"Fine."

Just then there was a knock on the door. George flushed.

"Do you mind if Inga joins us? You'll still have my full attention, I promise, but I need her."

What could I say? She was already outside the door. I rolled my eyes, which he took as an agreement and let her in.

Inga was tall and shapely, blonde haired, blue eyed and very pretty.

"Hi-i," she chimed.

She was already in her nurse outfit. I cringed, feeling utterly self-conscious, sprawled out before them both.

George opened a drawer and took out a box; when the smell of rubber filled my nose and my whole body tensed.

"Relax, June, it won't take long." I knew he and Inga were waiting for me, but I just couldn't shake the tension. After a moment's wait when nothing changed, George took matters into his own hands. I closed my eyes tightly, concentrating on music.

Five minutes later he was done. I sat up and Inga passed me a tissue to clean myself up with. She was smiling kindly and George was grinning at me with that self-satisfied, somewhat exasperated look he always got afterwards.

He leaned over and kissed my cheek. "Happy Valentine's Day, darling."

Then, turning to Inga, he said "Can you imagine how she'd be if she wasn't married to me?"

I scowled. "I'm going to work and leaving you two to it."

"She loves me really," I heard George say as I walked back through to the house. I smiled to myself. I guess there are worse things than being married to a dentist.

Playing Valentine's Day by the Rules
By Leigh Anne Jasheway

Once again, I present my annual attempt at trying to help men and those who would be men through the minefield of a holiday we lovingly refer to as Valentine's Day because "Sex for Chocolate Day" was vetoed by the greeting card industry. Valentine's Day is an awful holiday rife with meaning and emotion and totally devoid of football games, so it's no wonder it confuses most red-blooded American males.

Fortunately, I think I can help clear things up with the help of a few mixed sports analogies:

1. **Season.** Although it appears that V-Day is a single day (February 14th, for those of you who don't have the schedule memorized), the season starts on December 26th when the woman in your life goes to the mall to return the combination vacuum cleaner/thong you got her for the holidays. If you don't get in the game until the last minute, how can you expect to play as well as your opponent who has been scrimmaging for a month and a half?

2. **Tip-off.** You should be tipped off that the game has begun when your opponent says, "Honey, do you

know what day it is?" or gives you a pair of silk boxer shorts that say "Red Hot Lover" all over without breaking into uncontrollable laughter (remember, she's been practicing for six weeks!)

3. **Scoring.** You score not by scoring, but by making it appear that you're not even thinking about scoring. Here are two examples: (Wrong) You hand her a half-dozen half-dead roses you bought for $5 from a guy on the street corner on your way home and say "So, we gonna do it now?" (Right) You hand her a half-dozen half-dead roses you special-ordered from one of those hoity-toity flower shops for $80 and say "Why don't I put these in some water? Then I'll cook you dinner, massage your feet, and grout the tub like you've been asking me to for the past sixteen years."

4. **Type of Sport**. V-Day is not a team sport. Bringing your seven best buds over to watch women's volleyball will not give you the upper hand. This game is played man-on-man, by which I mean man-on-woman, woman-on-man, man-on-man, woman-on-woman, but never man-on-woman-while-all-his-scuzzy-friends-are-in-the-next-room-drinking-beer-and-hooting-at-the-TV.

5. **Penalties.** Penalties occur in any or all of the following situations:

Infraction	Penalty
You forget to buy her a card	Loss of dinner
You buy her a card and although you think it is hysterical, it makes her cry	Loss of heavy petting
Consumption of chocolates meant for her	25-yard penalty—you must remain 25 yards away from her until you do something creative and thoughtful, like superglue the toilet seat down, and offer to let her mother come live with you
You forget it's Valentine's Day altogether	Loss of sexual privileges for 6 weeks
You imply that she looks fat	Loss of manhood

6. **Offense**. The best offense is no offense at all. Sacking the quarterback midway through the seven-course candlelight dinner she prepared completely

from scratch will only leave you bruised, with the possibility of a groin pull, and wishing the coach had called another play. A "Hail Mary" approach is much better; sit there quietly eating dinner and nodding, while silently praying to every and any god that neither of you will be too full for you to get lucky later.

7. **Defense**. If your opponent begins to get aggressive too early in the game, play it coy. Say something like "You know, why don't I recite you this love poem I wrote for you instead?" Just in case she thinks you're actually serious, it's best to have plagiarized something by a famous poet earlier in the day. Avoid limericks and poems found in the men's room at the gas station.

8. **Instant Replay.** At several points during the game, your opponent may insist upon an instant replay. This can be quite a strain because most men don't have the stamina to be able to say, "I love you" and then turn around and do it again moments later. Vitamins or a well-hidden tape recorder may help.

9. **End of the Game**. The game is over when your opponent decides it is over. Her decision will be based on the number of fouls you incurred, any unsportsmanlike behavior, and whether you brought in cheerleaders to enliven the game. You should be

aware that many V-Day games end without a touchdown or home run. It happens to all guys once in a while and it's nothing to be ashamed of.

CONTEMPORARY CANDY HEART SLOGANS

BITE MOI
CAMEL TOES
BIG BORE
HARD UP
TOO TINY
NYET = NYET
DIE ALONE
NO PUBES
AMSCRAY
ICKY BOD
CALL 911
IT'S OVER
1000x NO
RUG BURNS
I'LL MACE
GET REAL
SHAVE BACK
TOUCHES SELF
R U DONE
JAIL BAIT
FIX TEETH

Holiday of the Heart
By Jackie Papandrew

Every year when football season is finally over, women have to begin the arduous process of focusing their men's attention on something far more important: Valentine's Day. There's a reason Cupid's commemoration comes so soon after the Super Bowl. It's an obvious test of the depth of men's romantic tendencies, and, sadly, it's a test they fail more often than a Cosmo relationship quiz.

My husband, God love him, is no exception. He will not become aware that it's time to pay homage to the holiday of the heart until he begins slipping on newspapers I place in front of the shower. As he steps out and ends up on the floor staring at a full-page ad that mentions Valentine's Day in a font large enough to be seen by the astronauts on the space station, a light will begin to dawn. It's taken a mere 20 years of this type of subtle training for my sweetheart to remember to pick up something special like a kitchen item we already have or an exquisitely wrapped collection of hotel toiletries. I haven't, however, always been so fortunate. One year, just after our second child was born, I received a bottle of stretch mark-treating cocoa butter clearly purchased last minute at the nearest 24-hour drugstore. This was accompanied by a box of Christmas candy with a 75-percent-off sticker and a card (sans envelope) featuring two kissing chimps. In an attempt to personalize the card, my man had tenderly tried his hand at poetry. Under his name, he'd written:

> Roses are red
> Violets are blue
> You want my body
> I know you do.

I've also received my share of ego-shattering lingerie, little bits of fluff that would barely fit the anorexic hips of a Victoria's Secret model. But the worst was a pair of silk pajamas - size XL -- that my husband brought back from a business trip to China. Designed for the smaller Asian woman, those damned PJs wouldn't go past my knees. I can tell you, nothing gets a wife in the mood for love more than struggling to fit into anything marked XL. I'm still in therapy over that.

My spouse has also tried to be sweet with scent. One year, he gave me two sample-size bottles of the same perfume worn by his mother for the past five decades. Big, big mistake. Another time, in a bid to impress me with his thoughtfulness, he procured a cylinder head from a World War II-era airplane (if you don't know what this looks like, consider yourself lucky) and created a lovely lamp that added a certain je ne sais quoi to our living room décor. It took me weeks to arrange an accident that sent this romantic piece of wreckage back to the junkyard.

I'm hoping that by our 30th or possibly 40th anniversary, my mate will have progressed to the point where he'll fill a vase with a single rose and a diamond necklace, or maybe the keys to a new Jaguar. In the meantime, I'll try not to lose heart.

MORE CANDY HEARTS

FEAR ME
I'LL HURL
GOT CRABS
OVER IT
NOT EVER
NO NECK
GET A PIMP
IN BRED
CUT ONE
TRY SOAP
I'LL DUMP U
GET OFF ME
I'LL YELL
FOR SALE
ZIP FLY
AS IF

Stock up the Car for Valentine Fail
By Mark R. Hunter

Yeah, so, I missed Valentine's Day this year.

On a totally unrelated note I've discovered it's possible, and even advisable, to sleep in today's smaller, more fuel efficient cars.

Well, I didn't totally miss it so much as I wasn't as prepared as I'd planned to be. I had this thought of cleaning up the house and setting up a romantic dinner with candles, and low music playing, and even cooking a meal myself. That last could backfire, as a trip to the ER is rarely romantic.

There are a few things I'm capable of cooking well, but they wouldn't make up anyone's idea of a romantic dinner: Macaroni and cheese, egg sandwiches, popcorn, mashed potatoes, and … actually, that's about it. There are some other foods I'm capable of cooking, but *not* all that well: hamburgers, a roast, and anything that boasts the word "microwaveable" on the box. I'm can also make a stake. No, that's not a misspelling.

The back seat of a car can actually be comfortable to sleep in, as long as you're the type who likes to curl up, or maybe if you don't mind hanging your feet out of a window. That's inadvisable this time of year. You may have to pad the seat a little, if it's got those little humps in it designed for making seating more comfortable.

That's totally unconnected to Valentine's Day, except that I should have put my fiancée into the car and driven her somewhere nice. I mean, *really* nice. I don't go out to eat often; if it doesn't have a drive-through, to me it's a fancy place. Applebee's is a formal affair.

Women don't see it that way. "Fancy" means someplace where they won't let you in without a tie, and I haven't seen a tie around the house since 1997. I think I used it to play tug-o-war with my daughter's dog, and if I remember correctly it was last used to anchor down my ladder while I was cleaning the gutters. The tie, not the dog.

Also, did you know you can't get a reservation fifteen minutes before arriving? At the restaurant, not the gutter. They actually laugh at you. They *laugh.* "It's Valentine's Day, and you want to walk in the door and be seated in half an hour? Ha ha. This is me, laughing."

The trick to sleeping in a car this time of year is staying warm. Now, if you work third shift like I do and sleep during the day, you can try parking the car in the sun and make use of natural heating, which works if there's not much wind. Have something to cover your eyes. It also might be a good idea to bring a snack, in case you can't get back inside the house.

The drawback is, of course, concerned passers-by and curious police officers.

You could also take an alarm with you. Once an hour, turn the engine on until the heater's warmed up, get it so hot inside the car that your mustache melts off (not that I'm talking about me), then turn the car off and sleep until the cycle starts again. This is expensive, and doesn't encourage good rest.

I tried to sleep in a parking garage once, and discovered the whole building shook whenever vehicles passed overhead. I kept dreaming of earthquakes.

Sometimes you can get yourself out of the proverbial doghouse with flowers or jewelry. This doesn't work for my fiancée; she's not a fan of either, except for engagement rings, and I already got her one of those. You'd think her dismissal of shinies would be a good thing. It usually is, but it doesn't help when the time comes for a quick gift, otherwise known as a desperate bribe. She loves books, but we've got so many books that I've been using them to insulate the car.

Not that you need insulation, if you learn my favorite technique for wintertime car sleeping: Simply park the car in the garage. Even if it's unheated, having that dead air space around the car will help hold heat in. A comforter under you, along with another over you, a couple of blankets, a winter coat, gloves, stocking cap, two pillows, and an empty jug in case nature calls, and you can maintain body heat well enough to sleep comfortably. This also helps avoid those nasty surprises such as passing semis blowing their horns, which can suddenly negate the need for the empty jug.

Or, you could just plan ahead for a romantic Valentine's Day.

I know what you're thinking: But Mark, couldn't you just sleep on the couch? Well, yes, but that opens you up to being kicked or doused with ice water by whatever annoyed female might be happening by. Or, worse case scenario, you could wake up with her pet snake crawling across your face.

Not that I'm worried about that. She wouldn't risk the snake.

Just the same … I'm thinking Valentine Sea Cruise, next year. I might end up sleeping on deck, but it would be warmer.

I was nauseous and tingly all over. I was either in love or I had smallpox.
Woody Allen

Valentine Verses
By Dorothy Rosby

Struggling to say just the right thing to your spouse on Valentine's Day? Try one of the following clever and sentimental verses I've come up with. Use more than one—if you think your relationship can take it. Just clip out the verses that are most appropriate to your marriage, glue them to a piece of red construction paper, and sign your name. Your spouse is sure to treasure your simple, homemade card as much as chocolates or flowers. But to be on the safe side, you might want to give those too.

Verses for your Valentine

> *For him:*

Darling, Love is a mystery! And so is the reason you put empty cereal boxes back into the cupboard.

To my very fit spouse, From this Valentine's Day forward, I promise to go the extra mile in our relationship if you will just go the extra foot. That's all it would take for you to carry your dirty dishes from the sink to the dishwasher.

Sweetheart, I'm so glad that we never let little things like whether the seat is up or down spoil our bliss. But if you forget to reload the toilet paper dispenser one more time, you can start going next door to use the bathroom.

To my big, strong husband, If anyone is tough enough to lift his dirty clothes off the floor and toss them into the hamper, it should be you.

To my favorite traveling companion, How I value your wisdom and support—except when I'm driving.

Oh baby, You're *hot!* But I'm freezing! Touch that thermostat again and I'll trade you in for an electric blanket.

Cuddle bug, I promise to stop elbowing you in the ribs when you snore—if you promise to stop snoring.

Dearest, You make me gloriously happy—some of the time.

My cute little couch potato, I could sit and stare at you cuddled up in front of the television all day. But one of us has to do the laundry.

Beloved, I promise to stop talking when you're reading the newspaper—if you promise to stop reading it at the dinner table.

For her:

Sugar dumpling, No that outfit doesn't make you look fat. Nothing could make you look fat. Now don't ask me again.

My fashionably late love, You look fine. The house looks fine. Now could we *go* already?

My fascinating Valentine, Yes I do listen when you talk. And talk. And talk.

Gorgeous, You look *stunning* in everything you wear. Why on earth would you need *more clothes?*

You're right, dear—*as usual.*

Love of my life, After all the wonderful years we've had together, I feel like I can almost read your mind. Now if I could just read your handwriting in the checkbook.

Sweetie pie, We make such a cute couple. I bet we'd look great in a duplex!

To my companion on life's highway, Of course I think you're a good driver. And with some coaching, you could be a *great* driver.

My sentimental Valentine, It's so cute how you get attached to your belongings. But shouldn't you give your old clothes to someone who can fit into them?

Happy Valentine's Day, honey! See I *do not* always forget!

MORE CANDY HEARTS

RU 18?

GET TESTED

I DO STANDUP AND IMPROV

THIS IS JUST A ROOFIE
I WROTE ON WITH A SHARPIE

Report Card
By Barb Best

Dear Connor,

Enclosed is your annual Valentine's Day evaluation. Comments will address key aspects of your holiday performance. When germane, I will reference concerns regarding the general progress you are making in our relationship.

✓ You receive above average marks on maintaining a positive attitude for most of the evening. We'll forgive (but not forget) the grumbling under your breath when I sweetly requested you serenade me with "Feelings."

✓ You demonstrated initiative and creativity (albeit with my constant prodding and direction) by making plum restaurant reservations for the mandatory romantic dinner. You exceeded expectations by donning the sexy, pink "lovebirds" necktie I gave you.

✓ You enthusiastically participated in the consuming of the extravagant calorie laden meal and (especially) the drinking of the inordinately over-priced French champagne. (Yes, I know you have suits that cost less than that measly bottle of hooch, but it was dang gauche of you to mention that while ordering.)

✓ Needs improvement. It is acutely evident that you need to work on the development of greater concentration skills (soup spoons are *not* percussion instruments) and on becoming a better listener (What? Huh? What did you say? Huh?)

✓ You really should not require repetition to retain such basic information as my profound feelings about cocker spaniel puppies and/or my deep thoughts on saving the planet from the calamity of cow flatulence.

✓ Your menu choices were a tad predictable (if not pedestrian) and mucho heavy on the garlic (spaghettini really!) Additional food note: Spinach is never a wise idea on a date. You know why.

✓ Bravo. You score big points for ordering a decadent dessert for us to share, then letting me wolf down the whole thing by myself. (I will forever cherish the memory of that heart-shaped, Cointreau-laced, triple dark cocoa crème mousse cake. Oh, My, God!)

✓ Gift Giving: Frankly, this is an area where I'd like to see significant improvement. I encourage you to fulfill your potential and aspire to a much higher level.

✓ A "V-Jazzle Home Kit" is not an appropriate Valentine's Day gift for a woman of my substance – even though you steadfastly insist it was a joke.

✓ Please remember that there is *nothing* – nada, zip, zero, NOTHING - *funny* about Valentine's Day. This is serious business, Mister!

✓ Gold Star: I want to commend you for admiring the gift of fine jewelry that I went ahead and purchased for myself with your Platinum Visa card.

✓ If you work hard on your organizational skills, I have reasonable confidence that you will be able to handle this difficult shopping task yourself at some point in the foreseeable future.

✓ Flowers: The red roses were okay, but you neglected to remove the price sticker from the crappy grocery store wrapper. FYI – Straight men are allowed inside florist shops.

✓ Recommendation: Embrace your metro sexual side and put a clamp on those (homophobic?) tendencies to avoid all things pink, pastel, and remotely namby pamby. (Yellow ribbons and coral orchids never hurt anyone.)

✓ Chocolate. Below average marks. Hershey's Kisses are kibble for runny nosed kindergarteners, not succulent aphrodisiacs potent enough to kindle the heavenly loins of your beloved sweetheart.

✓ Chocolate – Part Two. Hint: G-O-D-I-V-A has a web site that offers Double Cream Gourmet Truffles to cry for, plus emergency delivery. (They *love* Platinum Visa.)

✓ Kudos! You excelled in the demonstration of physical affection. You get an "A+" for effort. This is a strength you obviously take pride in.

✓ Please note that (being male) you can always benefit from listening, paying attention, and following instructions.

✓ I encourage you to work more slowly and accurately on this critical skill set. I am happy to meet with you anytime and tutor you.

✓ Plays well with others. (See "demonstration of physical affection")

I am happy to have you in my relationship this year and look forward to increasingly rewarding times together.

Your loving girlfriend & biggest fan,
Hugs & Kisses,
Kimberly

Reminder: My birthday is five weeks away. I'm sure you'll rise to the occasion.

Without Valentine's Day, February would be... well, January
   Jim Gaffigan

I claim there ain't
Another Saint
As great as Valentine.
   Ogden Nash

For that Special Someone
By Amy Bagwell

Did you enjoy your Valentine's Day? You know, that Hallmark holiday dedicated to spending too much on greeting cards that no one reads, flowers that will die in a week, and chocolates that no one wants to eat because the Christmas weight has yet to be lost? It is definitely one of those quasi-holidays that I celebrate more out of a sense of obligation than a true belief in whatever it is really about. I don't really know what St. Valentine did to achieve said sainthood, and does that in fact make it a religious holiday, and what exactly does it have to do with romance and love anyway? My kids get all up in the Valentine's spirit, wanting to know if their father or I want to be their Valentine. To which I say, "Ew. No thanks. Incest. Contributing to the delinquency of a minor. Statutory rape. Ugh." It doesn't sound like a happy Valentine's Day to me.

I suppose it could be argued that the reason anyone gives a crap at all about Valentine's Day is that Christmas is over and there is not a lot to look forward to for the rest of winter. The groundhog let us down once again, and the next big event is that Irish Catholic holiday dedicated to drinking. Come on, we all know alcohol is a depressant.

We are sick of the snow and the cold, and we are fatter and not ready to buy bathing suits. Face it, February sucks.

So instead of pushing off from shore on the nearest ice floe, we put all of our focus on February 14. We have yet to lose those extra winter pounds and would rather be hibernating, but instead, we pretend to be in love. Women actually shave that winter growth off their pasty white legs and squeeze themselves into garishly red, whorish lingerie. Men splash on too much cologne and make reservations for restaurants that don't even have beer on tap for a meal which will be slapped on an overdrawn credit card and paid off for months way after the last shrimp has been digested.

Wait a minute, that's not entirely accurate. Some men don't even realize it's Valentine's Day until they stop by the grocery store or the drug stores and have one of those "Oh Shit!" moments, grabbing the nearest thing they can find that is red or has hearts on it. But I learned last week that you have to be careful what you grab.

On Valentine's Day, my sister LM and I waited in the check-out line at "Your Valentine's Headquarters," the local Krewgers grocery store. In addition to the oversized mylar balloons and hastily arranged red roses with baby's breath stuffed in cheap vases in front of the check-out area, they had an interesting collection of gift baskets wrapped in cellophane on display along the registers. We saw one basket with chocolates and other gourmet edibles. We saw another with a bath scrubbie, some bubble bath, and a little packet of 3-minute mud masque. And we also saw one with a tube of K-Y Jelly and a box of condoms.

Yes, you read that correctly. They actually had a basket wrapped up with a small bottle of lubricant, a variety pack of Purex condoms (not to be confused with Purell hand gel, which offers a different kind of protection) and a couple of cheap champagne flutes. The only thing missing for the perfect Valentine's date night was the gift card for Red Lobster and a bottle of Tott's Brut. For the eternally optimistic, there was a basket also laden with rubbers and lube, but instead of champagne flutes, it held a matched pair of coffee mugs. Because sometimes you want to fall asleep in each other's arms and hold each other all night long. And sometimes you are counting the minutes before you search for your left shoe and your panties.

My sister and I were beyond delighted by the thoughtfulness of the Krewgers Floral Department, which had the foresight to create such romantic gift baskets designed to delight any couple in love, or at least lust. We could imagine how that went down.

Floral Department Manager: Gladys, we need you to make up some gift baskets for Valentine's Day.

Gladys: Should I get some of them fancy chocolates from the top shelf of the candy aisle?

Manager: Don't bother, just grab a couple of packs of condoms and put them in these old baskets we have leftover from Easter.

At least Krewgers was touting responsibility while promoting fornication. I was impressed those baskets were for sale in Cobb County, Georgia. I began to imagine other baskets they should have considered. Maybe one with a pack of Kleenex, a bottle of Vaseline, and a Star Wars action figure. Or perhaps one with handy wipes, a bottle of rubbing alcohol, and an over the counter package of Plan B emergency contraceptive. Or maybe one with a couple of cans of Fancy Feast and a copy of *Eat, Pray, Love*. A little something for everyone.

Last year, I was at Uber-Mart after Valentine's Day, and I scanned the clearance table looking for cheap chocolate. They didn't have any good dark chocolate, but they did have some leftover heart shaped candy boxes. They had the standard red and lace trimmed ones, and even a more rustic camouflage patterned one, but my favorite said "Get Er Done" real big on the front. If that didn't scream romance, I don't know what does. But honestly, I think Krewgers' love baskets win for creativity and directness. For $16.99, someone was going to have a happy Valentine's Day. Too bad we only celebrate that kind of special love one day a year.

I'll Take Willimance
By Jim Shea

Valentine's Day is about those five little words: Charge it to my Visa.

Romance has become a commodity. Saying I love you is no longer enough; now you must say it with something. So we:

Say it with flowers.

Say it with candy.

Say it with a card, jewelry, dinner or - for that really special someone - a Craftsman multi-purpose power saw with extra blades and a ... See what I mean?

Everybody is trying to cash in on Cupid's gig. One of the most blatant attempts, though, has to be from Amazon.com, which earlier this week came out with a list of "The 20 Most Romantic Cities in America."

Before addressing which cities are on Amazon's list, let me just name a few that aren't: New York, New Orleans, Los Angeles, Chicago, Portland, Denver, Santa Fe, Boston.

Boston! Can you imagine leaving off Boston? Is there a more romantic place in the country - in the world, for that matter - than Boston on a Saturday night in July when the Yankees are in town and you have Green Monster seats and reservations at Remy's afterward? I mean, hose me down.

Frisco did make Amazon's list, but not San Francisco - Frisco, Texas. I'm sure Tony Bennett is reworking the lyrics to his signature song as we speak.

Some of the other cities that made Amazon's top 20 include such romantic garden spots as Cincinnati; Round Rock, Texas; Ann Arbor, Mich.; Clarksville, Tenn.; Dayton, Ohio; Gainesville, Fla.; Murfreesboro, Tenn.; and the winner, Alexandria, Va.

To truly understand the lameness of Amazon's list, all you have to do is check the criteria on which it is based: sales data of romance novels and relationship books, romantic comedy movies, Barry White albums and sexual wellness products.

If these criteria prove anything, it is that the cities are not the most romantic; they are the least romantic. What we are talking about here are places where large segments of the population are sitting around reading about romance, watching movies about romance, grooving to music about romance and doing God knows what with their sexual wellness products instead of getting out there and getting it on.

I'll take romantic Willimantic any day.

(Editor's note: Willimantic motto: We have flush toilets).

How to Say "Be my Valentine": Let Us Count the Ways
By Kate Heidel

As ridiculous as it may sound, clubbing a man over the head with a bat and dragging him into your love den has been interpreted by people who belong to fringe groups like the "police" and the "courts" as somehow criminal. What in heaven's name is a girl to do?!

We at *Happy Woman* want every one of you to score a valentine this year, so we've whipped up the perfect workarounds to ensure that you get some loving, and not 5 to 10 for "aggravated assault," whatever that means.

Pizza Delivery Gal

There is no law that we know of against delivering pizza any time of day or night. Like a sexy detective, uncover what pizza shop your object of desire orders from. Slap their logo onto the side of your car (free advertising!) and bribe one of their high school delivery boys into giving you his silly pizza hat—it's your ticket to love!

Now order some pizza for carry-out and slip it into the pizza tote you bought from amazon.com for only $40. (What price love?) Buzz your soon-to-be fella in his lobby.

Remember, ladies: no man alive will turn down pizza, especially if he didn't order any. Besides, what man could resist your siren song of pepperoni over the intercom? Just think Marilyn Monroe as you purr, "I'm here with your pizza, darling!" If the lobby sports a security cam, all the better, you slinky exhibitionist. Pay no mind to the building manager; they all carry cell phones and pretend like they're calling the police.

Wake-up Call Gal

What man doesn't want a chipper voice on the other end of the phone to ease him into his busy work day instead of a clunky old alarm clock? For that matter, how about a relaxing voice at the end of the day to send him off to bed at night? And an efficient voice at noon offering all the latest lunch specials within walking distance of his office? Using your imagination and 600 favorite photos of lover boy tacked onto your inspiration wall, you'll think up hundreds of perfect reasons to call him and make him realize he simply can't function without you! Remember our Happy Woman motto: "Be consistent and persistent!" Don't miss a single call and don't let a little thing like a secretary or a restraining order throw you off course—he's just playing hard to get!

Mail Carrier Substitute Gal

Legally you're not supposed to impersonate a federal employee, but that can't possibly extend to faux subs looking for love! With the rope you've set aside for hanging yourself should things not go as planned (very last resort!), climb the tree closest to your heartthrob's bedroom window and then swing on in to give mail delivery that personal flair. If honey's not home, add your own love note to his otherwise humdrum stack of mail and thoroughly tear up anything that might distract him from your words of ardor. You can use it as bed confetti! It's those little touches that gets a man's attention, ladies!

Free Lawn Maintenance Gal

There certainly can't be any law against pruning bushes or mowing the lawn! Imagine his delight as he turns into the driveway after a grueling day at the office only to find you, the future light of his life, with a gleaming pair of pruning shears in your gloved hands! Pay no attention to his gallant protestations as you fire up the lawnmower and carve a love message into the grass. Forget-me-nots like "Please be mine" or "If I can't have you, no one will" are sure to quicken his pulse, the precursor to passionate romance! And because you know how to make a lasting impression, slip a blood-red rose behind his ear while refusing payment for services rendered. Now that's lawn maintenance with a love-time guarantee!

More Effective than eHarmony!
By Sarah Garb

Are you single this Valentine's Day? Well have no fear—take some love advice from third graders and you'll be dating in no time! They have vast experience, what with the steady stream of love notes, the budding playground relationships, and the partner dancing in P.E. As Lucas once put it, "Third grade has turned into LOVE grade!" The actual quotes and notes below will guide you through every relationship stage from pick-up lines to break-ups.

The Pick-Up

If you're just starting out in your relationship quest and are looking for that all-important pick-up line, consider taking a cue from Tyson's note to me one day in my teacher mailbox. "How come you are not married? You are beautiful and stuff." That is practically *guaranteed* to work at a bar or your next singles kickball game. What woman doesn't want to be called beautiful? And stuff?

Compliments are another surefire way to get the conversation rolling. Take this one from a confiscated love note: "My sister thinks your dad is hot!!" Total turn-on, right ladies?

Another note-writer hit upon what I think is a pretty fail-safe conversation starter with the object of your affection. "How are you doing? Fine? Sexy? How?"

Definitely be direct. Whoever said that revealing your true feelings has to be any more complicated than a few well-placed hearts? Simply replace any vowels in the name of the person you're after, and it's practically a done deal. To guarantee, though, that this sentiment is made crystal clear, you would do well to model your email headings after Jalil's note to Savannah.

> To: S♥ v♥ nn♥ h
> From: Jalil
> Date: March 6th
> Time: 10:12 am
> Reason: I want to let you know I like you!

When you're really putting yourself out there, you'll want some confirmation that the feelings are mutual. The best way to achieve this is undoubtedly the "circle yes or no" option. Followed by a threat.

I really like you because you are the most prettiest girl I ever seen.

Would you like to be my girlfriend yes or no.

P.S. give back on the way back from recess.

Don't let nobody see this or you are dead.

If Rebuffed

Dear Daniel,
I broke up with Steven. Do you like me?
yes or no
from Becky

Much though we'd like to think that the "circle yes or no" will result in a yes, there is the potential for a circled no. If this happens to you in your quest for love, as it did to Becky, do not be dissuaded! The appropriate response in this situation is to insult the other woman and question your crush's taste. Anyone out looking for love but finding "no" can certainly take a lesson from Becky's last-ditch effort to change Daniel's mind.

"Emma has freckles and she is so ugly. How can you like someone so ugly?"

Breaking Up

Let's face it--breaking up is a fact of the dating world. It's difficult to know just what to say, but these elementary suggestions can help you find an effective approach. Why make it any more difficult than three simple sentences?

"I don't love you. I love Trevor and Marcus. But I kinda like you."

And if it has to be done, Michael has the perfect way to let someone down easy.

"I'm not really into girls. I'm more into Godzilla."

Ways To Say "I Love You"

English........... I Love You
Spanish.......... Te Amo
French........... Je T'aime
German.......... lch Liebe Dich
Japanese....... Ai Shite Imasu
Italian............. Ti Amo
Chinese......... Wo Ai Ni
Swedish........ Jag Alskar Dig
Eskimo.......... Nagligivaget
Greek............ S'Agapo
Hawaiian....... Aloha Wau la Oe
Irish.............. Thaim In Grabh Leat
Hebrew......... Ani Ohev Otakh
Russian........ Ya Lyublyu Tyebya
Albanian....... Une Te Dua
Finnish......... Mina Rakkastan Sinua
Turkish........ Seni Seviyorum
Hungarian... Se Ret Lay
Persian….…. Du Stet Daram
Maltese…..….. Jien Inhobbok
Catalan…..…. Testimo Molt
Redneck .… Nice Tits

Hearts and Bubbles and Tiny Pink Candies
By Patty Friedmann

I whispered to Him. "Would you like to know what's really going on with me?"

He got a little pale, as I knew he would. We had a tacit understanding. We were beyond intimate. Best friends, lovers. But things worked between us because neither of us had a deep secret longing to get married and live together. At least I assumed so. I thought maybe he was afraid I didn't.

"You think I don't know what's going on with you?" he said.

"Not my cardiac function," I said.

His entire body went limp with relief.

B is my primary care physician. Our relationship is top secret because doctors can't be involved with patients—especially married doctors. He knows all my numbers; he's listened to my heart with a stethoscope. But I wanted more. More!

I wanted an echocardiogram. I was a spoiled kind of mistress.

"It's the perfect Valentine's present," I said. He was happy to agree. What more could a man with a romantic streak give a woman--and a gift that would be covered by insurance? Especially insurance that I carried only because I was holding onto my latest marriage until I got Medicare. The gift reeked of symbolism.

His voice was soft and loving. "Your heart will be perfect," he said. "I can guarantee it."

He liked my healthiness. He ran around like crazy seven days a week because he had an aging patient load, and the only problem I'd ever presented was a huge toxic bite by my cousin's mean cat. He probably also liked fooling around with a woman who was more fit than I should have been at my age.

But I wasn't so sure. My father dropped dead on a Caribbean cruise, and without an autopsy we'd had to assume it was his heart. My mother didn't learn her lesson, and a quarter of a century later she, too, had died on a cruise. At least she'd died a little more slowly, having fallen down because she had atrial fibrillation. With that kind of heredity, I should have bet against B on my heart.

Sure enough, he was sufficiently wrong that I should have questioned his medical judgment. Or at least his prescience. I had something called an atrial septal aneurysm. ASA among the cognoscenti.

Whee! An aneurysm!

I was secretly thrilled. An aneurysm sounds life-threatening. B was upset. Everyone I told was upset. And the more people I upset, the more people I told. I was like a little kid who fakes a limp, and the more she gets attention, the more exaggerated the limp gets. My heart, my heart. I was doing a Fred Sanford. Of course, I also was doing a lot of poking around on Google. B said that finding an answer on Google was like getting a teaspoonful of water from a fire hydrant. All he could tell me was that atrial septal aneurysm, when coupled with something called a patent foramen ovale, put me at risk for a stroke. PFO for short.

What a bonus a stroke was. I'd gone into this whole adventure with the attitude of a born cynic: I wasn't lucky enough to die young. So through and through I didn't believe this problem was going to kill me. "Hey," I'd say as I played the great stoic, "I think a stroke would be a splendid gift. Frankly, I have no aversion to sitting in a chair and staring into space all day. I already see my faculties pinging off the screen one by one as it is."

Anyone who is still my friend is generally tolerant of my attitude toward life.

B was worried. He wanted me in the care of a cardiologist, and Dr. M was the best in the business. "I'll be seeing a very fine cardiologist in a couple of days," I said dramatically to all the people who were inquiring earnestly. B did want to know if I had the PFO that raised my risk of stroke. By that time I was hoping I had one, because I'd already told a half dozen friends and relatives that I had the ASA/PFO combo, and they all had access to Google as much as I did. If I didn't have the PFO, I was going to be just a regular person with an aneurysm which wasn't as interesting as it sounded.

Dr. M was sure I didn't have a PFO. But she set me up for a bubble study. I loved it. A bubble study! Hearts and bubbles. It had all the makings of a whimsical greeting card. They were going to inject saline solution into an IV, and when it reached my heart, a sonogram would monitor to see whether bubbles went through between my heart chambers. If it did, it meant I had a PFO. A PFO is a hole that should have closed after birth.

A young associate watched the study. "Bubbles," he said. "See the bubbles? I'm sorry." Then he left the room. It was a Friday, and I had an entire weekend of e-mailing to do.

I actually felt crappy. When I got down to it, I really didn't want to lose my faculties to a stroke. I'd always said that I didn't need my mind because I had my attitude. But the truth was that I'd kind of gotten attached to my mind.

B was also kind of bummed out. He was very tolerant of my being depressed. He actually was a man who didn't mind knowing what was going on with me.

Dr. M phoned on Tuesday. "How are you?" she said.

"I don't know," I said. "How am I?"

"You're great," she said.

I didn't get it.

As it turned out, the ASA/PFO combination wasn't all that scary. At least the way mine looked to a skilled cardiologist. All I needed to do was take a baby aspirin every day.

A baby aspirin! A tiny pink candy from a little bottle with a pretty red heart emblazoned with a happy numeral 81. Taken each day with a sweet cup of tea. The same protection I could have chosen if I'd read some article in Reader's Digest or watched Dr. Oz.

But that wasn't the point. B had given me a couple of weeks of great fun. I'd forced people to consider the possibility that I might die. Or worse, that I might be reduced to a severely compromised version of my regular self. It wasn't as good as seeing my own obituary, but it was close enough. I even got to see B worry about me. Love on Valentine's Day. All in all, I highly recommend an echocardiogram as a Valentine's gift. Even if it's going to come up with a normal reading, you can tell everyone in somber tones that you're going for heart tests. Good mileage to come from that alone. Except from the poor doctor who knows better. Next year he'll probably do flowers. If he puts up with my foolishness that long.

Husbandology
By Robert G. Ferrell

With Valentine's Day staring us smack in the face again, it's time to change the water in the goldfish, put a new flea collar on the minivan, and rotate the cat. As husbands good and true, we should also take this annual opportunity to reflect upon our love lives by giving ourselves a frank scorecard for the preceding year. Did we bring our wives flowers for no reason at all, or only to plug those little leaks that got sprung in the dike of matrimony? How many times did we compliment the little woman on her appearance/culinary skills/home decorative acumen/wrestling moves? Did we snap at her when we should have been supportive? Did we duck in time? Little things like this add up and can make or break a rib...er...relationship.

Keeping a wife happy is not as difficult as some have postulated. (My home remedy for postules, incidentally, is a balm of one part olive, two parts vermouth wrapped around a large gin and applied liberally to the afflicted area.) It really just entails paying attention. If your wife comes home from a hard day of shopping and excitedly shows you coupons she found for a free entree at a local restaurant, do you: a) wisely take the hint and suggest that you eat out tonight; or b) ask her what's for dinner and sleep on the sofa? Take your time and think about it. I'll be over here sweeping up those potato chip crumbs you dropped around the couch the last you failed this exam, you slob.

Another way to put husband points up on the board is to answer questions correctly. In order to be successful at this, you must first understand that wives employ what appear to us to be simple inquiries in the same manner that those bug-eyed gray aliens use mind probes. "Does this dress make me look fat?" is the probe for a husband's Honesty Calibration. For example: If you answer in the negative, the wife will instantly seize on what to her will be the glaring unspoken implication that other components of her wardrobe do not share this salubrious slimming effect. In other words, when you say, "no," she will hear, "no, not that dress." We won't, for the sake of the squeamish among us, discuss the consequences of answering, "yes." The only relatively non-toxic response to this question that I've run across is, "no dress could make you look fat, dear."

Wives continually lay down obstacle courses for husbands to run. This is genetically programmed into them, probably as some ancient defense mechanism against hairy grunting pursuers with clubs and low manual dexterity. The key to navigating them without getting mangled is to swim with the current, rather than against it (although this is roughly equivalent to avoiding getting hit by any blowing leaves during a windstorm). What lends these soggy broken-field exercises an even more difficult aspect is that they can be both topological and conversational in nature. Allow me to develop this argument further (fair warning: I have developed arguments in the past to the point that they are issued their own ZIP code).

Women periodically set forth on furniture-moving expeditions that defy all male attempts at explanation. Any item of home furnishing, up to and including huge commercial stainless steel walk-in refrigerators, can and will be relocated on a regular basis by even the most petite wife—one who otherwise has difficulty lifting a roll of garden hose without spousal assistance. This behavior is deeply ingrained and there is probably nothing we as husbands can do about it. We would be foolish even to try.

I once came to visit my widowed mother while I was off in college (and I was off practically the entire time) to discover that our monstrous built-in range, which had seen its best days during the Truman administration, was out in the storage shed, leaving a gaping hole between two counters in the kitchen. "How in the world," I asked her in disbelief, staring at the wide gulf bristling with metal hoses and other severed arterial connections until recently occupied by the enormous appliance, "did you wrestle that thing out of here and down the back porch steps by yourself?" Sitting at the table sipping her coffee, my five foot-five inch, one hundred-thirty pound maternal parent answered, simply, "one step at a time, baby."

A significant result of these periodic self-imposed Herculean labors is that the collateral debris from the disinterments tends to appear in places we as husbands do not expect there to be any such obstacles. Men are, above all else, creatures of habit. I start my day at 0515 each morning and begin the horrific process which eventually leads to my sitting at a desk thirty-two miles away slaving away at an utterly pointless job that nonetheless pays so well I can't bring myself to give it up. (At least until I sell so many books I no longer need to make that daily pilgrimage into perdition. You are cordially invited to assist with this noble goal.) I don't turn on the lights in the morning, partly because I don't want to disturb my exquisitely light-sensitive wife and partly because I can never remember which switch does what. I don't need illumination, though, because I have the long, complex path to the kitchen (we have a very large, rambling home) memorized down to the last grout bump between floor tiles.

In the immediate aftermath of a full-scale furniture relocation spasm, however, there will invariably be small, dense, impossibly dark objects scattered along my accustomed path. While in the friendly light of day they may appear to be nothing more than planters or decorative fabric-covered doorstops, inert and harmless, in the pre-dawn hours they assume the mantle of the infernal. Negotiating these suddenly treacherous waters successfully often exceeds by a considerable margin the severely diminished capacity of my slumber-sodden mental state. As a result, when I finally do make it to the kitchen to get my coffee I will have, at a minimum, three new abrasions, a jammed toe or two, and possibly even torn slacks. Even when the latter catastrophe has befallen me, I know better than to try to make that journey back again to replace them. Better to bear with the ills we have than fly to others that will surely lacerate us further.

If I make the very grave mistake of confronting the wife about it, I will unwittingly steer myself directly into the verbal half of the aforementioned steeplechase.

"Honey, why did you leave all that stuff in the hallway last night? I nearly broke my ankles trying to get to the kitchen."

"Why didn't you just turn on the light?"

I'm already backed into a corner here, as I don't want to admit I can't remember which switch it is.

"I didn't want to wake you up, darling."

"I was already awake, sugar. You were making a lot of grunting noises."

"How could you hear those? I know I wasn't that loud."

"They echoed."

"Next time, could you just leave a clear path to the kitchen, please?"

"Next time, turn on the light. You shouldn't be stumbling around out there in the dark every morning, anyway."

There is no graceful exit from this.

Valentine's Day also reminds us to keep abreast of the simple things—holding the door for your wife, pulling out her chair (resist the temptation to wait until she's already committed to sitting down), telling her how nice she looks without being prodded (one of my favorites: she brings you some object and asks, "what do you think of this?" You grasp her waist tenderly and reply, "that's beautiful, darling—and the [object name] isn't bad, either." This one is a guaranteed winner: you owe me), and doing thoughtful little things around the house like rinsing your dishes and putting them in the dishwasher, taking out the trash before the health department shows up, and mowing the lawn while the back fence is still visible from the house—are all effective non-verbal ways to tell your wife, "I love you very much, darling. Please don't put salt in the sugar bowl again."

Saint Valentine (there were actually at least three of them, historically) is traditionally associated with romantic love and an exchange of gifts between intimate companions. Interestingly, there is little-to-no evidence that Valentine (any of them) really espoused a connection with this theme during his (their) life (lives). A lot of the rituals we now associate with Valentine's Day were fabricated by greeting card companies, with confectioners and lace-makers cheering them on from the sidelines.

Chaucer seems to have laid the foundation for our modern conception, although the content of his poem on Valentine's Day (something about birds looking for mates) suggests he was thinking of St. Valentine of Genoa, whose feast day is May second, rather than the one we now call St. Valentine, as mid-February in England is no time to be looking for anything except a wool blanket to hide under, preferably one situated in front of a roaring fire.

Shakespeare was all over Valentine's, of course. It may be a bit difficult to extract for modern audiences, but there's a lot of romance and intimacy, or at least an intimation of intimacy, in The Immor(t)al Bard. The Elizabethan psyche, if the popularity of Shakespeare's tangled syntax and even more tangled plots serves as any indication, was obviously the direct forerunner of our modern fascination for word puzzles, Sudoku, C-SPAN, and assemble-it-yourself furniture. The complete works of Shakespeare have been translated into at least thirty languages. Sadly, English is not among them.

Returning at last to our topical topic, intrepid husband, ask not what Valentine's can do for you, but rather what you can do for Valentine's—and it better be good for her, if you know what's good for you.

Ciao, amore.

What the world really needs is more love and less paperwork.
Pearl Bailey

Falling in love is so hard on the knees.
Aerosmith

Love is what you've been through with somebody.
James Thurber

Love is an electric blanket with somebody else in control of the switch.
Cathy Carlyle

On Feet Beating & Valentine's Day in Iran
By John Boston

"She plucked from my lapel the invisible strand of lint — the universal act of women to proclaim ownership."
— *O. Henry, 1910*

Normally, I'd be the first to applaud police wandering about with long sticks, whacking celebrants of that most heinous of all holidays, Valentine's Day.

It's today, you know.

I'm a romantic fellow. My sweetheart is a romantic lass. We are constantly showering each other with treats, gifts, flowers, cards, notes and compliments.

But come Valentine's Day, we stubbornly boycott.

Valentine's Day is manufactured romance. It's poetry for the dim-witted. It's 10 million cow-eyed elementary school teachers dully knifing through construction paper, slopping on paste and doilies and calling it art.

Worse, it's gender-biased.

Valentine's Day is all about girls, mush, things pink, guilt and cooties.

Still. In my Crabby Appleton acrimonious bile-filled heart, I can find no place that condones what those grumpy, soapless muftis pulled off in Iran.

They banned Valentine's Day.

According to The Associated Press, hard-line Islamic grumpybutt clerics in their hotel bathrobes issued an order. They told the Iranian Fun Police to close down any shops primarily in the wealthier northern part of Tehran that were hawking Valentine's Day merchandise. Any card sporting a heart or kind sentiment was yanked from the shelves. About the only greeting card left was:

> Roses are red,
> The Ayatollah is great,
> Have fun at the prom
> With a goat as your date.

Or:

> Forgot your card,
> I'm as red as a beet
> The fundamentalist police
> Were beating my feet.

Actually, I might pop $4.95 for a greeting card like that if when you opened it up it played that tinny little Arab melody to: "There's a place in France where the ladies wear no…"

Well.

You know…

"…Foster Grants."

One Iranian café owner was threatened with jail if he hosted his advertised Valentine's Day party. Teddy bears with hearts, candies, bouquets and certainly anything in English that said, "You Are My Dweam Boat" were banned by the ultraconservative Muslim clerics who oversee the police of that country.

"For weeks, I've been waiting for Valentine's Day to offer my boyfriend a gift of love and affection," a 19-year old girl named Altena told AP. Smart cookie Altena is, she didn't give her last name. I'm hoping Altena is about as common a name as Ashley-Heidi-Brittany is in America. "The crackdown only strengthens my position in rejecting the hard-line clerical rule."

Actually, the ridiculousness of the enforcement underscores the division within that country between hard-liners and reformists and moderates. It also put me in the uncomfortable position of rooting for Valentine's Day.

Well. In Iran, at least.

My big gripe with V.D. is that it's terribly skewed toward women, although I think there are a few guys out there who enjoy celebrating Feb. 14.

I think they're called, "Sissies."

Out of the 365 slots in the calendar, you'd think there would be a male equivalent day of rejoicing, one that does not involve florists or fruity high-pitched songs that make dogs howl.

"Loving You" by Minnie Ripperton comes to mind.

Here. I've memorized the lyrics:

"La la la la la. La la la la la. La la la la la. La la la la la. (pause) La la la la la. La la la la la. La la la la la. La la la la la."

Take a deep breath.

"La la la la la. La la la la la. La la la la la. La la la la la. (pause) La la la la la. La la la la la. La la la la la. La la la la la."

All of you across America reading this essay who feel Minnie Ripperton should be publicly stoned and beaten with shovels for her international anthem to Valentine's Day, raise your hand.

Let's see. One, two, three, a million, a billion. Sorry, Minnie. You didn't make it.

I've oft lobbied for a 24-hour period to be dedicated, a day where the manly man is celebrated.

And you know how you women could do that?

Leave us alone. Just leave us the hell alone. That's all. Don't knit us a baseball cap or make us breakfast in bed. Don't make reservations for tea at a cozy bed and breakfast. Let us sleep until 2 if we want. Let us wander the streets in our underwear, dazed, with our little tummies hanging out. Let us scratch our heinies on trees. For those few of us males who are A-type driven personalities who feel the need to get up at ungodly beach-assault Normandy landing hours to play golf or play hockey on Guy Valentine's Day — fine.

Let us do it.

No. Really. I mean, "Let us do it."

As we're stumbling out of the house to go hunting or shoot mail boxes, don't give us one of those terribly predictable put-upon sighs, reeking of feigned nobility and patience.

Don't roll your eyes like some comic hen. It's not sexy. The waitresses at Hooters don't plant their hands on their hips, purse their lips and roll their eyes. Neither do The Bud nor Laker Girls. If you want to do something useful, go have a smoke, watch Oprah and learn a few Spanish verbs to share with the maid while we're gone.

Some of us will want to spend Guy Valentine's Day eating 40 or 50 chili dogs with a pal. Some will want to play 35 holes of golf, collapsing before the 36th hole so completely Irish blottoed that even the fairway sprinklers hitting us full-face at 3 the next morning won't revive us. Some men will want to stay in the garage on Guy Valentine Day, just drilling holes or throwing knives while humming The Green Beret Ballad.

Now there's a song. "Silver wings, upon their chest. These are some, of America's best..."

Women — let us have our day.

Don't even look at us. Don't look in our direction because if you do, you'll spoil Guy Valentine's Day for us. If we're face down in the gully, gathering our strength after some monumental drunk, don't pull us out. A rain will come along shortly and we'll eventually float somewhere safe. We're guys. We know what we're doing.

Don't bail us out of jail. Don't even ask how our brief 24-hour furlough went.

Secrecy is a top component of Guy Valentine's Day.

This is just a guess, but I'm thinking that thousands of years ago, they had a successful Guy Valentine's Day in Iran. Over the centuries, the women of Persia started slowly eroding the holiday by whining "I wanted a giant pink stuffed panda with 'I Wub You,' written on its belly, only in Farsi," or "You never take me anywhere. I wanna go to Solvang for the weekend."

And that, pretty much, is how extremist Islam was born...

I 🖤 V-DAY
By Cammy May Hunnicutt

A comic take on Valentine's Day seems about right to me: I seem to remember it being about comics from the get-go. And not in all that good a way.

It seems like Valentine's would be the perfect day for little girls, doesn't it? Getting cards with pink hearts and white lace and all the rumored sugar and spice. But looking back on my Southern girlhood, what I always picture is little boys taking advantage of the opportunity to come up and give me what I now interpret as sexual hate mail. And there were always comic strip characters involved.

The whole thing on Valentine's was bizarre enough in grade school, anyway: they made us pick names out of a decorated hominy can to see which member of a much-despised gender we had to buy cards for. Think about that a minute: here's this declaration of love—whatever that might mean to grade school kids—and it's chosen by luck of the draw. Your love life settled by random lottery. I'm not sure that situation improved much later, come to think of it. Now I have 736 "friends" on FaceBook, all chosen by random cyber-bumps. And half of them are males with Muslim names sending me sexual hate mail.

So I'd sit there in my little integral desk/chair opening envelopes with chocolate fingerprints (or worse) and here'd be this flimsy Five & Dime card with the obligatory red ♥ and Garfield making some tacky comment. I mean *Garfield*? This fat little cat with his insinuating hooded eyes, which even in my short season of innocence I saw as dripping with too-knowing, carnal smugness. And he wants to be my Valentine? What, this grubby little boy is just a messenger to bring me this *billet-dou*x from the king of corporate fatcat commercial tie-ins? But of course it would be personalized on the back. As personal as you'd want to get with seven year old boys, anyway. Something sweet like "Girls are booger butts", or "I hate Cammy's gopher gutts."

I stayed away from kids since I quit being one myself, but I'm sure the comic characters progressed. Little Mermaid, right? Belle from The Beast? What do they have these days? Sponge Bob? Vampires? Pirates of the Caribbean? Speaking of Mr. Depp, were there Edward Scissorhands valentines? Then why not Freddy Kreuger? And if you're getting into famous pop manicures, why not toss in the Wolverine? The Three Musketeers of LeeNail slashcry aspire to your heart. I'm sure there were Dilbert Valentines. As absurdly inappropriate as it gets. Cathy? Did Ren and Stimpy make it? Monsters Incorporated? I'd have grabbed up some monstrous eyeball over Garfield in a hot second. But you think about it, who was the first comic Valentine? Who's this Cupid with his phallic little arrow? AKA "Eros"? From which we derive so many useful terms that are pretty over the top for love messages to eight year olds.

But the thing is, whatever the girls were in it for, there was no doubt what the boys were after. All after that famous One Thing, right? Exactly—candy. Personally I thought Valentine candy was shoddy compared to Easter, which was just around the corner. Rabbits with biteable ears, white chocolate Fabergé eggs covered with Viennese swoops and little dioramas inside, jelly beans (with "belly jeans" cracks from my brother Powell) And Cheeps! I loved stuffing those little shmallow chickies in my cheeks. I scarfed them up so bad Powell told me I'd turn into a marshmallow myself. And pinch my puffy little waist to make his point. So who turned out to be a model and who turned out to be a chubby chemical salesman with love handles even Cupid couldn't get a grip on, huh? I ♥ you, too, Pow. Show you how cool HE was about Peeps, he made these Kentucky Fried smores out of the poor little things. But I have to admit, they were finger-lickin' good.

But V Day candy, well... Oh sure, the boxed collections: Whitman's Samplers, those clinical See's wrappers and heart-shaped boxes of little Forest Gump surprises, not too shabby.

But there's something about eating hearts, don't you think? I mean why don't we just build big sacrifice pyramids? Maybe it's because I was into my Girl Scientist phase at the time (and how I went from future Madame Curie, Tomb Raider to Loose Lingerie Model is a story in itself, but let's save it for my cautionary memoir) but the whole idea of chowing down on sticky red facsimiles of human organs didn't do much for me. But it was okay, because in there with all the white lace and false promises were these little hard candy hearts with funny slogans on them. Valentine funnies, see? An idea whose time has long since come. People think Twitter is cool with their 140 character limit, but somebody was out there, trapped in a Chinese cookie factory or somewhere, communicating true ♥ with only a couple of words. I used to fight with my sisters, high-grading out the good ones to give to people. Stick little Bethany with all the lame ones like "Bee's Knees" and "Hep Cat".

But some of them seemed pretty cryptic. I remember one said, "You Rock". And I was like, what? "Me paper, scissors"? Or "Them Eyes". WTF? "Come On" didn't seem that racy at the time And what does "Get Real" have to say? Go get your own real, sport. I had my eyes out for one that said, like, "Aorta". Or "Transplant Me". They didn't have any that said "U Bite Boogers 2" or anything useful, but I figured out I could just make my own. The first literary project of my life was licking words off little pastel hearts and writing in my own slogans. With toxic ink, now that I think about it, but that was in keeping. So I was actually doing rewrites prior to being a writer. I had some great ones, like, "Boys Barf" and "Blood Feast" and "Be Dead Now" and "Your Face, My Butt" and they went over reasonably well, In fact Raeford Cole snatched a bunch of them up and put them in his mouth all at once. When I was making a second batch, secretly pleased that Rafe and his pals had eaten something I had licked on, Gram caught me at it and went into one of her Old Testament seizures. Snatched up all my literature, jabbering, "That mess is *toxic*, Camelia May. Meaning it's pure poison and could do a body harm. You're whipping up a plague here." Which tickled me to pieces, though it turned out Rafe never even felt poorly. But it's interesting (or maybe prophetic) that my first public writing was turning candy into hubba messages to boys. And that they didn't even read them, just gobbled them up.

So what you really have with Valentine candy is that it's all packaging. Regular old candy pimped out paper moon romance so people will get all gooey about what's essentially just chow. Speaking as somebody with way more experience of sexy undies and cosmetic artifice than even most women, and more secrets than Victoria, I'd have to say that's a major metaphor there. Like somebody said, "If love is blind, why is lingerie so popular?" A major reason not to go all teddy/bustier/crotchless/chiffon for your designated love toy on Valentine's. Some intentions are best read by braille. Not that anybody sells anything more pertinent, like little heart-shaped snap-top tin boxes of lubricant. Bottom line, so to speak: *candy,* you nitwits. Lay in some chocolate hearts or whatever bodily organ seems sufficiently inappropriate. One thing little boys and big girls see ♥ to ♥ on.

ROMANCE MATHEMATICS

Smart man + smart woman = romance

Smart man + dumb woman = affair

Dumb man + smart woman = marriage

Dumb man + dumb woman = pregnancy

Nip it in the Rosebud
By Karla Telega

Still don't have a date for Valentine's Day? You could troll the church socials and clambakes for just the right guy or gal—one that will not be a source of laughter and derision among your friends for years to come—or you can always depend on modern technology.

Personally, I don't trust online dating services. It's human nature to exaggerate our good qualities, and downplay the fact that we occasionally urinate in the closet. Would you really move in with someone if you knew that your shoes were going to be in the splash zone? Before you spring for the flowers and naughty jammies, take heed of these first-date warning signs.

She thinks the moon landing was a hoax

A popular theory among paranoid schizophrenics and residents of New Jersey. With proper treatment and heavy medication, both conditions can be managed. She'll pinch the Valentine chocolates to make sure they're not all coconut and suspect you of using her toothbrush to comb your mustache.

He has made multiple appearances on Jerry Springer

His ex-girlfriend accused him of dating her dog behind her back. If he is served with a summons for a paternity test during the appetizer, don't stick around for dessert. RUN!!!

Her purse weighs more than she does

She took the designer dog fad to an extreme and adopted a designer Rottweiller. She obviously has trouble with spatial relationships. Don't under any circumstances allow her to park your Porsche. Prepare to spend Valentine's Day in the emergency room getting your arm reattached after you try to hold her hand.

He walks his cat

Single men who own cats are immediately suspect for deep emotional problems. They thrive on rejection and indifference and have the phrase "fear of commitment" tattooed on their backs. If he puts his cat on a leash, he has obviously lost touch with reality. You can expect to spend a romantic Valentine's dinner in separate restaurants.

Her last boyfriend was a mime

She has serious communication issues. Trying to break up through normal means (never calling her back) holds little meaning for her. Surprise her on Valentine's Day with conversation hearts that say, "I'm moving to Iceland."

He wears his pants backwards

He is anatomically confused and will not know which end of the hose goes in the spigot. If you want to end Valentine's Day on a high note, you'll need to draw him a map and break out the hand puppets.

She wants you as a partner on a reality show

She will do anything for her 15 minutes of fame. If this involves setting any of your body parts on fire, she will not hesitate. Make sure you have a good supply of Aloe Vera on hand.

Hopefully, you won't encounter any of the above dating train wrecks. If you already have that significant other, this is the time of year to cherish her or him. You could do a lot worse.

The Great Negotiation
By Rachel Turner

My first Valentine's Day as a newlywed, my husband drove all over town looking for a copy of *The Notebook* because he knew how much I wanted to see it. We popped popcorn and snuggled up on the couch and watched it after we came back from our nice dinner out that he had planned. I also got flowers and chocolates. I think we would all agree that he did well.

In return, I gave him a pack of gum. It came with a card.

He was a little offended.

"Meaningful Valentine's Day gifts don't come from the drug store, Rachel," he declared after realizing the unequal thought that went into the planning and execution of this lover's holiday.

I was ashamed and very glad I failed to mention that the gum was in fact buy one, get one free and purchased as an afterthought at the register. I inconspicuously pushed my own pack further down in my purse and tried not to look as guilty as I felt.

So early on in our marriage, I mistakenly thought Valentine's Day was a girl's holiday…just like when we were dating. I was wrong.

It was not my first public display of thoughtlessness.

At our joint wedding shower the summer before, we played a game to see how well we paid attention to the other one. We were asked all of these questions that would determine what we knew about each other. He scored a 24 out of 25.

I got a 4 1/2.

I got the half credit for declaring confidently that the car he drove when we first met was a "red one".

Flash forward a few years and add a child into the mix and you get Valentine's Day planning conversations like this one:

"Valentine's Day is next week." I declare one February evening after my beloved husband arrives home from work and is just settling in with a beer and a sports recap of the day.

"Yes. What did you want to do about that?" he replies completely disinterested and not looking up from *Sports Center.*

"Maybe we should do presents." I suggest.

Oh no. He has nothing planned. He's not even nervous that he forgot about Valentine's Day. He's lost his will to be thoughtful.

"Okay, but if you buy it while waiting for a prescription…I'll know". He looks directly at me.

He can't remember weekend plans, but you buy one pack of gum and he never forgets.

"Right…no drugstore gifts." I agree not wanting to start something.

"Nothing that is 'As Seen on TV' either." He adds. "I have no need for a Ped Egg."

"But it removes dead skin and you can zest a lemon with it." I argue only half joking.

"Rachel."

"Fine, but you would have loved growing that Spongebob Chia Pet with Sam. That's a father/son bonding opportunity missed."

"Look, let's sidestep this potential landmine right here and now. I have $50 in cash on me. Why don't you take $25 and I'll take $25 and we'll just go buy ourselves something that we really want." He reaches for his wallet and hands me the money.

"Great idea. Pedicure, here I come," I say as I inwardly sigh in relief. No gift buying pressure this year.

Then he has an idea. "Why don't you buy some lingerie?"

"Ugh…what kid of Valentine's gift is that?" I ask as I count my money to make sure it's exactly $25.

"It's not for you. It's for me. I like lingerie."

"Then go buy yourself some." I suggest flippantly.

"Valentine's Day is about being romantic and even sexy. I like lingerie and you never wear it anymore. I don't even remember the last time you wore it." He remarks.

"July 23, 2004." I supply.

"Really? That long? Why?"

"Because that was the day I swore to myself that I would never suck in again. The fact that it was also the last day I wore lingerie is purely a coincidence" I lie.

"That was during our honeymoon." He states.

"Right. So?" I question.

He shakes his head in disbelief "Well, I liked the lingerie. Couldn't we have discussed a decision like this? It does affect me." He thinks for a second. "You know what I like to see you in."

I roll my eyes, "Please say my blue sweatpants."

"You mean that cotton birth control that has holes in the thighs? No."

"You refer to my blue sweatpants as birth control?" I fold my arms across my chest.

"Well, you didn't have them until after you gave birth and if you'll notice, Samuel is still an only child."

"That's nice."

"You are my wife. I love you very much and this will be your gift to me. Besides, if you do buy lingerie, I'll never bring up the Valentine Trident incident again."

This type of deal interests me greatly, but I'm not quite ready to strike a deal.

"What happened to the $25 plan? I was totally fine with that being our Valentine's Day gift."

He stares at me long and hard enough to make me wonder if he is secretly digging a tunnel somewhere behind a Rita Hayworth poster that he will one day crawl through, buy a bus ticket to the beach and live out the rest of his uncomplicated life with Morgan Freeman.

I then take a moment to reflect on the potentially bitter custody battle we would have over our beloved living room furniture and decide once and for all that there's no need to needlessly split up a matching couch and love seat. There are too many broken homes already, so I relent.

"Fine. I'll buy some lingerie."

He smiles. "Really?"

"Yes." I reply.

"That's great, thanks honey."

"How far up do I need to shave for this?" I ask.

"This is getting too complicated," he sighs. "We'll just make tacos and watch shows in different rooms like every other night."

"No, it's Valentine's Day…we should do something as a couple. To keep our marriage strong."

"Why? I'm not going anywhere."

"That's so sweet." I flutter.

"Sweet? Look, I finally convinced your mother that I don't like mayonnaise. I don't want to start that conversation over again. That alone took the last seven years to accomplish."

"So that's more important to you than lingerie?"

"No, it's just the only battle I've won around here." He goes back into an ESPN trance.

I think for a second.

"Fine. I'll do it, but here are my terms. I'll buy the lingerie, but I'll buy it with your money, not mine, and *I'm* picking it out. You can pick the color, but I retain all color veto rights. I'll wear it, but only between 9:30 and 9:36 on Valentine's Day night. There will be no encores. These are my terms."

He stares at me. "Fine, but it has to be above the knee, can't button up to the neck and no robe."

"Done." I agree.

"Oh, and absolutely no 1800's style puffed sleeves." He adds.

"Fine, then I will not consider anything with the world 'edible' in the name and it has to have a crotch. Also it will absolutely not be a costume to dress up as anything with the word 'naughty' in it."

"Anything else."

"No. Yes. The lights have to be off."

"Then what's the point?"

This is a valid argument, unfortunately. "Fine, no *direct* lighting. Do we have a deal?" I hold my hand out to the love of my life.

He looks at me for a moment and nods.

We shake on it.

I kiss him on the cheek lovingly, "Happy Valentine's Day, honey. I love you. Now, I'm going to get that pedicure."

I flit out the door, very proud of my negotiating skills as I hear my husband grunt and settle back down to his beer.

Who says the romance dies when you get married?

A young woman was taking an afternoon nap. After she woke up, she told her husband, "I just dreamed that you gave me a pearl necklace for Valentine's day. What do you think it means?"

"You'll know tonight," he said.

That evening, the man came home with a small package and gave it to his wife. Delighted, she opened it--only to find a book entitled "The meaning of dreams."

Love Amongst the Nudists
By Dawn Weber

February 14th. Flowers for the women, sex for the men, and everyone goes to bed mildly content.

I mean, happy.

I don't want flowers, romance or sex on Feb. 14. You know what I really want?

A nap.

Because:

A - I'm tired, and

B - My motto is Valentine's Day: Who Gives a Shit?

When you're single, it sucks because…you're single. I have been there, and nothing screams "I'm sad! A loser! And possibly a sexual predator!" like a solo V. day.

All the happy couples, going out to dinner, dancing, blah, blah, blah.

And the single folks stay at home. With boxed wine and battery-powered "massagers."

Bachelors and bachelorettes, I'm here to tell you - chin up. It is not dinner, dancing and XXX blah blah blah. My husband and I have been married 16 years, we have two kids. Our Valentine's Day isn't all fancy dinners and fireworks. No sir!

It's Applebee's. And Netflix, if we can stay awake.

That's why we decided to mix it up a little bit this year, taking a trip to Key West, Florida over the Feb. 14 weekend.

And there, at the Garden of Eden rooftop bar entrance, I found two words that made for a, um, different Valentine's date night:

"Clothing Optional"

Intriguing! This meant I could "opt" to keep my clothes on, while others - perhaps young, attractive males - would "opt" to remove theirs. Mammies for the husband, franks and beans for me.

Everybody wins!

Now, now, I am not a total perv. Please understand this: Boobies abound. Men can catch glimpses of coconuts in movies, magazines, prime time TV, the city bus...

But it's, um, harder for women to get a peek. Sure, the husbands offer to show us the ol' Thrill Drill (constantly). But can't a girl sometimes look at different twig 'n berries, in the same way a man views other fun bags?

Also, my Garden of Eden curiosity wasn't completely rooted in naughtiness, because the place also advertised itself as a "dance club."

Let's picture that, just for a minute: naked...people...dancing. Thingies...bouncing..all about. The bobbing hilarity - it made me smile.

Yep. Nudity: The gift that keeps on giving.

Knowing that my husband - like most men - loves looking at the milk jugs, I showed him the sign.

"Look, honey," I said. "'Clothing Optional.' Maybe you'll see some hooters!"

"I don't know...that's kind of weird for me...and there could be naked MEN in there..." he said.

Exactly! I thought.

"No way!" I said. "Dudes wouldn't do that. And it's our Valentine trip – let's do something crazy!"

"OK...but I don't know about this..." he said.

We began climbing the three flights of stairs to the rooftop bar.

"Honey, I really don't know about this..." he repeated.

This is a man who has seen me give birth to two children, so nude that he probably saw my internal organs in the delivery room. It was something I didn't even want to witness.

"C'mon - you can handle it!" I told him.

We climbed another flight.

"I really don't know about this..." he said.

He is also a guy who has body-bagged three-day-old bare corpses, found dead in their bathrooms.

"You'll be fine! You're tough," I told him.

We reached the top.

Two young men, buck naked and fast-dancing, straight ahead. Franks and beans bobbing hither and yon, just as I'd hoped for, er, I mean, imagined.

"Aaannndd I'm out," said the husband, turning around.

On the right, more nude dudes, sitting and chatting to fully-clothed women. Very few naked females.

In fact, the weenie-to-coconut ratio tipped far in my favor. It might have been a gay bar, but I didn't care.

Ding-dongs are ding-dongs.

"OK! I'll be downstairs in a little bit!" I said, waving goodbye.

I settled in for the show, carefully not touching anything, and smiled on behalf of women everywhere.

Hey - it wasn't your typical Valentine's date. But it beat the hell out of Applebee's.

Yes, That's Right, I'm normal

By Jason Offutt

My wife sometimes worries me. Not the normal husband worried, like 'will I wake up tomorrow?' It's a deeper, darker, more rational worried, like when she comes home from the library with a book about relationships. Coming home with a book on Valentine's Day has DEFCON status.

I'm actually writing this from the fetal position.

"I'm reading this book," she said, catching me completely off guard by starting a conversation. She knew I was trying to hide because I hadn't bought her anything romantic ... yet. I hadn't bought her anything romantic *yet*. "It's about the differences between men and women."

It's at this point in movies the man, played by somebody like Paul Rudd, looks at the woman, played by somebody like Jennifer Aniston, and says something smarmy that in real life would see him on the street holding a suitcase with a knife in it. I'm smarter than that.

"Wanna watch TV?" I asked, hoping to distract her.

"No," she said, brushing me off. "I think you should read it."

There are six things real guys don't do:

1) Use napkins.
2) Watch movies like "Titanic," "Chicago," or "Phantom of the Opera" unless there are ulterior motives involving getting naked on the couch.
3) Hold your purse in the mall.
4) Talk.
5) Think about Valentine's Day earlier than noon on Valentine's Day. Then it's only out of fear.
6) Read books about relationships.

Actually, there are a lot more things real guys don't do, but I'm saving those secrets for *my* book on relationships, "Men Are From Mars So Back Off, I'm Holding a Ray Gun."

"Uh," I said. "Okay."

Then I got the look that meant if I were Paul Rudd my suitcase would have a nuke in it.

Guys, as we know, women are under the misconception that we're difficult to understand. As we know, we're not. If women were a mathematics equation, they'd be trigonometry. If guys were a mathematics equation, we'd be addition of no more than two single-digit numbers. We like to build things, destroy things, do things that involve cars, balls, sticks or other hitting things, and watch things explode on TV.

Period.

"But you're going to read the book, right?" she asked.

This is when I hit the fetal position where I remain to this moment. It really is comforting. You should try it the next time your wife talks to you.

Doesn't she know me better than this? I wondered because the only book on relationships I've ever read involved a monkey and a man in a yellow hat. And nothing good ever came of it.

Ladies, guys don't like to think about things that don't involve pork products, beer and cheerleaders. Even if a guy is a physicist, trust me, he doesn't like to think about things either. Pondering the mysteries of gravity is fine; why it wasn't acceptable to tell your wife that, yes, her butt does look big in those jeans is not.

"Of course, honey," I said, and escaped to work. As a college instructor, work is where I say things and people write them down, occasionally ask questions, but never ask me how I feel.

At some point in the day my phone rang and I was foolish enough to pick it up. It was my wife. Had she been back to the library? Has she checked out "The Secrets of Male Weeping," "A Complete Guide to Man Musicals," or even worse, "Your Guy Loves Cuddling: And Seven Other Things He's Afraid to Tell You"?

"Hi," my wife said. She sounded astonished because she was. She'd read something so disturbing, so alien to her, so profound, it shook her core belief system. Then she said those words all men hope to hear from their wives, but aren't optimistic enough to expect.

"*You're normal,*" she told me. "I've been reading the book and you're just ... normal. Guys don't talk to other guys about their personal lives. Guys get offended if someone suggests they need help. Their way of showing compassion is to punch another guy in the arm. They don't like to go shopping and they all like sports. I can't believe it, all this time I thought maybe it was just you, but all guys are like that."

If I weren't such a guy, I may have teared up. Maybe books on relationships aren't so bad. Next Valentine's Day, I'm getting her a book on small engine repair.

True Love—Then and Now
By Eve Gaal

Poem At Twenty

Valentine, my sweet,
Your eyes they sparkle so,
I wonder if you realize...
Their impact do you know?

Valentine, my dear,
Thy heart is oh so kind,
Its value almost measures...
The brilliance of your mind.

Valentine, oh Valentine,
You're everything to me,
The clouds, the sea and mountain air;
Forever may you be.

Valentine, my Valentine,
Stay forever as thou are,
Thine eyes, dear heart and lovely soul....
Unmatched they are by far.

Poem At Forty

Valentine my loving gal,
Your touch and kiss so sweet,
Will you still love me
When you realize I cheat?

Valentine, your rear
Nothing will surpass-
In fact I have to smile,
When I think about your ass.

Valentine you really shine,
When my buddy's come to town,
And even though we smoke cigars,
You never wear a frown.

And Valentine, Oh Valentine-
I know I'm not a monk,
But you always love me anyway-
Even when I'm drunk.

Valentine, my Valentine-
I love the tight pants you wear,
And even though you're gaining weight,
I love the way you swear.

Valentine, my Valentine,
There's no one else for me,
I will give you all of mine,
If you could just do this one free.

Five Things I Will NOT Be Doing on Valentine's Day to "Please my Man"
By Blythe Jewell

1. Squeezing into slutty lingerie

I don't dress up to have sex. If naked's not good enough, we have a problem. Besides – lace chafes.

2. Sensual massage

I have really weak fingers and wrists.

3. Scattering rose petals around the bed

Somebody's got to clean that shit up, yo.

4. Cooking an elaborate meal

If you had ever seen me trying to Forrest Gump my way through the kitchen, you'd understand that I'm actually doing him a favor with this one.

5. Feeding him chocolate-covered strawberries

Any chocolate in this house belongs to me, exclusively – regardless of the occasion.

Look. I love my guy, but I don't need a special day to be awkward, uncomfortable and falsely selfless. That's what dating was for.

On Giving Her a Japanese
Garden Trowel For Valentine's Day
By Michael Andreoni

If another civilization of semi-sentient life were detected living microscopically in the residue at the bottom of our coffee cups, would we find them more difficult to understand than our own kind? A caffeine-based race of aliens from a coffee bean galaxy, the Starbuckians (well, what would you call them?) could at least communicate to us, without much in the way of argument, how they like their coffee. We might easily understand their preference for, say, a large Double-Mocha with extra froth, over the Petite Espresso taken black, by simply counting how many were swimming around in each cup.

I find myself envious of such easily achieved communication this morning. Of straight-forward demonstrations of "I like this, I don't like that." Gazing into the bottom of my cup of cold comfort, I'm keen to initiate First Contact with the Starbuckians, to pry out their alien wisdom for the good of my species.

"Oh my little friends," I murmur, hoping none of the other café patrons enjoying their magic elixirs overhear me talking to a paper cup, "How go your lives, and do you marry? Have you ever, completely innocently (or completely unconsciously), given your partner a gift that caused her eyes to blaze with a fell light that pierced you with their baleful glare? Has, just for example, the phrase "Clueless Lummox," ever been applied to you in a pitying tone? And how did you get out of it?"

I need answers on this cold winter's day, a plan of action for escaping the regretful pall weighing heavily on me. If I can piece together exactly what went wrong, if I can list my errors as a warning to others, then perhaps something might be salvaged from last night's horror. When I fell from grace over what is already permanently imprinted on my cerebellum as "The Unfortunate *Hori-Hori* Incident."

The Starbuckians might tell us that love among humans is an odd phenomenon, a too complicated dance, performed blindfolded, compared with the matter-of-fact romances of the rest of the animal world. They could cite the example of Trumpeter Swans, which mate for life, but so far as anyone knows do not feel called upon to present their darlings with thoughtfully romantic gifts every fourteenth of February. They build their nests and raise their fuzzy little swan-lets without losing any feathers over whether a bit of dried seaweed is or isn't the most affectionate symbol of undying devotion. If they give gifts at all, any old thing would seem to do just fine.

It might require a more sophisticated race then our own to point out that a finely made gardening tool can be romantic, and I wish a Starbuckian would jump out of *her* coffee cup and tell her so this morning. I wish it would whisper that the Japanese do not mess around when it comes to garden tools, that all the latent skills of a people who once equipped the Samurai with the finest swords in the world went into the *Hori-Hori* she rejected violently last night.

No overgrown tangle of vegetation could frustrate its ten inches of forged surgical steel, mated for life to a handle precisely milled from the hardest hardwood to be found on the Asian continent. A blade that makes short work of irritatingly deep-rooted dandelions, but is also fully capable of giving the North Koreans something to think about should they be foolish enough to invade while an avid gardener is stabbing weeds.

That said, it must be admitted that love expressed through gardening tools is risky. There was a certain amount of doubt in my mind as to what she really meant when she presented the catalog and proclaimed "It's wonderful! It's just what I want!" I took a look at the picture, and was properly skeptical. I had learned, I thought, that usage and context are everything in these matters and that connecting "Wonderful" to something which exists to root around in dirt could be perilous.

"Oh come on," I scoffed. "You don't really want me to get you this, do you?" I knew she couldn't be serious for I had history on my side—my history, unfortunately. The memory of the chilly reception given to a barbecue grill presented on the auspicious occasion of her fortieth birthday was still very fresh, as was the contempt shown for my agonized plea of "You said you wanted one!" As well, the bitterly regretted Dim Sum cookbook, an unwelcome ghost of a decidedly cold Christmas past, warned of the penalties for guessing wrong again. No, I wasn't to be fooled this time. A romantic something *would* be found—I could never be stupid enough to give her, on Valentine's Day, a fancy weed-digger.

It's a funny thing (though not quite so amusing this morning), the way that ideas which are laughable a month before a deadline become more and more appealing with each passing day. I sneered at the catalog straight through the last days of January, confident that something better would suggest itself. It wasn't as though I'd never achieved the complex alchemy of the right gift given at the right time. I bolstered my self-esteem with memories of her beautifully twinkling eyes reflecting the glittering jewelry of years past, her joyful squeals over surprise vacation trips. No man can be wrong every time and expect to go on claiming half of the marital bed. The logic was comforting: I was still married; therefore I'd had a few victories and was at least as good as other men. Which, as it turned out, meant exactly squat.

The problem was that yesterday's brilliant success is hard to copy. No one can stand in the same river twice when it comes to presents, which, like nuclear weaponry, are a perpetual quest for the newest, the biggest, and the best. The gold bracelet that delighted her last year would not work again unless this year's selection sported diamonds. And should I choose to live really dangerously, next year's gold bracelet had better be adorned with jewels looted from a Pharaoh's tomb. I knew all that. I also knew my credit cards would not stand that level of escalation. Biggest and best were out, newest would have to do.

All through that first week of February I searched. I remember it only dimly now as an increasingly frenzied montage of flash-edited scenes of my hands pawing through catalogs of every description. They Googled countless variations of "Romantic And Affordable Valentine's Gifts She's Never Heard Of And Will Worship You For." There weren't really any results returned that met all the criteria, though some of the x-rated products were interesting, and if I had been able to believe their manufacturer's claims, would have come close.

By Sunday afternoon I was a wreck. Confidence gone, avoiding eye-contact with my wife, I complained, around seven o'clock, that I was really, really tired and slunk off to bed. There to mull my options and avoid, as best I could, thinking about the Doomsday Option: "Dear, I couldn't find anything good enough for you." A moment's prescience revealed the direction my life would take after such a gambit and I lay shivering with terror under the blankets, my life-force ebbing away. Anything would be better then that. A few tired looking grocery store roses, twin ferrets on a leash, chocolate covered balloons—all infinitely better then appearing before her empty-handed.

It was time for honesty. I'd struck out big and there wasn't much time left to do anything about it. I ran through the dozens of possibilities I'd rejected as too expensive, too clichéd, too this, too that. Was there anything I'd nixed too quickly? Anything I'd never given her before that didn't cost a fortune? Well, yes. Yes there was.

I'd never given her a Japanese garden tool. The idea of it was revelatory. In the history of the world, probably no one had ever given a Japanese garden tool for Valentine's Day—even in Japan! I would be the first. That this seemed a good thing to me is illustrative of the distant and dark place my reason had fled to during that stressful week. I had lost my way in the quest for a perfect gift and there, in the gloom of my darkened bedroom, this most feeble glimmer offered hope of rescue. I just wanted... needed the ordeal to be over.

That my wife had put the idea into my head was most appealing. She'd placed the catalog before me and asked… no, *demanded* a garden tool. She had done this several weeks before Valentine's Day, which, I was proud of being smart enough to recognize, was a hint that she wanted it *for* Valentine's Day. I'd be doing what she wanted, wouldn't I? And, I asked the ceiling, if that wasn't the essence of romance, what was?

I was suddenly giddy and had to get up and walk around the room to burn off the energy surging through me, rejuvenated by the knowledge that I'd cracked the code. I flicked the light on and spoke aloud into the mirror: "To hell with the ferrets! I spit upon stinking ferrets. I spit upon wilted grocery store flowers and inedible chocolate balloons." I would bask in my wife's admiration by giving her the perfect romantic gift. The bedroom could no longer hold me. I had an order to place.

The Starbuckians have failed me. What is the use, I'd like to know, of inventing an alien race if they won't do what I want? I've sat in this café (and really, the décor is quite ugly, greens and browns—ugh!) all morning, pleading for their help. People are looking at me and I don't know if I can stay much longer. An overly officious manager-type has gathered a protective screen of barristas around her, pointing them toward me like attack dogs.

And still the Starbuckians refuse to answer! I wave my cup around to shoo away the coffee clerks and stir up the stubbornly mute aliens. Maybe a good shaking will make them understand I'm not playing.

I've told them my sorrows and now I want the use of their greater wisdom to answer a few questions: I would like to know how everything went wrong so quickly. I want to know where the *hori-hori* landed when she threw it out the back door into the garden. Most of all, I would very much like to know if I can go home yet. Her birthday is less then two months away and I'll need every minute.

Rejected Valentine Cards

Here's some candy. Get in the van.

Very few puppies were injured making this card.

I want to cut off your face and wear it like a mask.

You're purely a Platonic friend, with maybe a little Hume and Descartes thrown in for taste.

My Sci-Fi Valentine
By E. Mitchell

Hellen had planned a picnic out by the lagoon. Though a lagoon in the middle of the Nevada desert was rather unusual, so was a fifty-foot spider. I had ceased questioning the whys and wherefores associated with such a surreal place. I was concerned now only with the whosits and whatsits.

"Who's your little whosit?" I said coyly to Hellen as she unfurled a blanket by the edge of the lagoon.

"Who's your turtle dove?" she replied flirtatiously, mimicking a lyric from a popular song of the day. Mercifully, rock 'n' roll would soon be sweeping the nation.

"Isn't black an unusual color for a body of water?" I inquired, surveying the lagoon.

"Not for a toxic waste lagoon."

"It's kind of romantic," I said, as the smell of sulfur filled the air. "Ever go boating?"

"Too corrosive," she replied matter-of-factly. "My canoe disintegrated."

"What about swimming?" I asked

"Why not skinny-dipping?" she added. "Who needs skin?"

It was a provocative remark. It was hard enough to picture her without her lab coat much less her skin. I had trouble keeping my mind on the conversation after that.

"Bla bla bla bla," she said.

"The beauty of nature is quite a distraction," I interrupted, brushing a two-headed toad off the blanket we shared. "Hellen, what I'm trying to say, what I've been trying to say since the first moment we met is, I want to see you naked, I mean I love you."

"What did you say?"

"My love is naked," I improvised hoping to avoid an overturned picnic basket on my head, or a possible dunking in the toxic lagoon. "My feelings are exposed. I'm a scientist not a grammarian; choose whatever sentence construction you like, the word naked is in there somewhere, but in a good way." She hadn't tossed anything at me yet so I felt it safe to move closer. "Though our devotion to science is what brought us together, it's also kept us apart. For just one impetuous moment forget about science, take off that lab coat and swim cap, and throw caution to the sulfury winds."

The moment that every man dreams of had finally arrived – a woman was buying my line. I felt a sense of empowerment unequaled since my membership application had been accepted at Vic Tanney's gym. Of course that had been a clerical error. But now as Hellen reached to unsnap the rubbery chinstrap of her flower-festooned bathing cap, nothing could cast a shadow on the magic of the moment.

Suddenly a giant shadow shattered the magic of the moment. As if in slow motion, I watched in horror as a web-footed behemoth emerged from the lagoon and snatched Hellen away in front of my very eyes. And before she had even had a chance to remove her lab coat! The creature raced off in the direction of the desert with Hellen's cries growing as faint as my hope of ever seeing her again, especially without her clothes on.

Without delay I sought the help of the Colonel, who at this point was refusing to take my calls. Only after a televised news bulletin reported sightings of a fifty-foot monster heading toward Las Vegas did he concede to help. He couldn't resist the promise of complimentary shrimp cocktails.

Since the monster was traveling on foot, albeit an enormous foot, we stood a good chance of beating it into town. This would give us time, not only time to cordon off the area, but also to see a quick show. Not that some scantily-clad show girls could take my mind off what's-her-name the scientist, but it was worth a try.

"I forget, why are we here?" I questioned the Colonel as we exited the dark casino back into the glaring sunlight.

"Shrimp cocktail," he replied.

My memory was restored as reality intruded. The piercing shrieks of terrified onlookers alerted us to the arrival of the monster. Hellen's screams were the first clue in locating the beast, as well as his bulbous head towering over the buildings of the Las Vegas strip.

The creature was still clutching Hellen tightly as he peered into hotel windows, terrifying the nubile feminine occupants inside. For the first time I tried to put myself in his shoes and realized there was an upside to being a mutant.

His freakish size was menacing. Ponderously, he ambled along the thoroughfare leaving destruction in his path. He tossed automobiles like playthings after ransacking a toy store. He disconnected a telephone wire and used it to floss his teeth. An uprooted palm tree made a decorative parasol.

When he reached a footware display, he longingly fondled an enormous replica of a shoe but then tossed it down in frustration when he realized it would be useless without an enormous shoehorn.

"We've got to do something," I implored the Colonel.

"Before he destroys any more property?"

"No, before Hellen gets mad at me."

"We've got enough fire power to do the job," the Colonel reassured. "My men are in position to take aim, but we can't shoot until he puts the girl down."

"I've got a plan," I said, grabbing the bullhorn. "Put the girl down so we can shoot you!" I shouted at the monster. He failed to comply.

"Got any other plans?"

As we argued about strategy, the monster loped away from the strip heading in the direction of Boulder Dam (renamed Hoover Dam in 1947 after President Boulder was impeached). We took off in hot pursuit as the temperature soared to 105 degrees. At least it was dry heat.

Our desert chase ended at the observation deck of the Hoover Dam. There wouldn't be time to pick out souvenirs as the giant stood perched precariously over the edge of the plunging waters.

"Put the girl down so we can kill you!" I shouted once more through the bullhorn. This time my plan worked. The monster released Hellen, and the Colonel's men opened fire. We watched in awe as the colossal creature tumbled, misshapen head over massive heels, into a watery grave below.

"T'was beauty killed the beast," I waxed poetically.

"No, it was an automatic weapon," the Colonel waned pragmatically.

All in all, not the worst date I've had on Valentine's Day.

On Valentine's Day...
Tell her how you Really Feel
By Mike Mulhern

Remember Valentine's Day when you were a kid? Those were the days. You would bring a stack of cards into school and the teacher would make you write one to every member of the opposite sex in class, even the ones who had cooties.

(I'm not sure this practice even happens in schools anymore. Probably because all it takes is one kid with runaway dandruff stuffing envelopes to cause a major anthrax scare.)

Back in the third grade I had a crush on a girl named Holly. That year I made a special heart to enclose in my Valentine card to her. It was made of red construction paper, had an arrow going through it and a message: "Be Mine, Holly!" I watched her expectantly as she opened my envelope, removed my special heart... and immediately burst out laughing. She looked over at her friend, scrunched up her face in a grimace and tossed my heart aside.

The next year I made another special heart for Holly. This one had a bullet ripping through it, red bloodstains spattering the inside of the card and the message, "Die

Holly, Die!!!" That led to the first of several visits to the guidance counselor in my academic career.

Through experiences like this I have become something of an expert when it comes to Valentine's Day cards. So I'll do a service to all the guys of the world. To help the lost, the lovelorn and the lovable losers out there with their sweeties, I've devised a list of common Valentine phrases and what kind of message each one really gives to the recipient. Because obviously when it comes to Valentine's Day cards I know how to send a message.

Be Mine

A good solid term to use in a Valentine. Bespeaks directness and confidence. Has a little touch of being commanding too, like you're a borderline stalker—chicks dig that. Don't use the word "Please" at the start though. You don't want to look as desperate as Jennifer Aniston at a Chippendale's dancer convention.

You're Everything To Me

Avoid this at all costs. Needy, needy, needy! Gotta maintain some sort of independence, guys. However, if you're already at the point where you're eating vegetarian *and* organic, you may as well use it—you were irretrievably whipped years ago.

I Love You

Simple, classic… and boring as hell. You better come up with something better than this, fellas. This is Valentine's Day, not kissing your wife goodbye before work.

You Have My Heart

This is not a good one to use. Never cede ownership of your heart like this. If your divorce ever gets messy you may not get it back.

To My Soulmate

Very heavy stuff here. Proceed with caution! Once you breach the "S" word there's no going back. Saying you love someone is nothing compared to that. Everyone says "I love you" without meaning it nowadays. It's like saying "bless you" after sneezing.

Bless you

Oops, sorry. My soulmate just sneezed.

I'm So Glad I Found You

This is a nice thing to say… but almost too nice. It sounds appreciative and more cordial than it should be. Makes you sound like you lucked out big time in finding a girl. You don't want to sound fortunate; you want to give the impression you bagged her like a ten-point buck during hunting season.

You're The One

A great phrase to use. Makes women gush. Sounds very nice without being specific enough to lock you into a position. After all, "the one" could mean anything. Such as: "You're the one... girl I met who doesn't immediately start dry heaving at my body odor."

Finally...

Die Holly, Die!!!

Pretty much speaks for itself. And if you do use it, say "Hi" to the guidance counselor for me.

Candy, Cards, and Coupling
By Saralee Perel

On Valentine's Day, we think of cards, flowers, chocolate, and of course something else. On this cold February day, our senses come alive as we engage in our utmost desire: spending 2 hours on Facebook. Sorry. I didn't mean that.

I meant to say: " . . . our utmost desire: chocolate almond ice cream."

No I didn't.

What I really meant was, well, you know - something I have difficulty discussing. I'll use the formal medical terminology: doing "it."

My immaturity around this subject has been a lifelong problem. Most of us have that memory of walking in on our parents. I quietly came into their bedroom to say I was having a nightmare and wanted to sleep in their bed. I was twenty-two.

I stood there, stunned, wondering, "What was God thinking? Shouldn't procreation be a little easier? These contortions look like something even David Copperfield couldn't get out of."

Do you remember your parents telling you about sex? Could you believe it? I still can't. When my mother took out a book filled with pictures, and then showed me, I freaked out. "This is disgusting! I'm never doing this!"

Then I had an incredible realization. "Not you and Dad! You two did this?" Before she could answer, I thought about my older brother. "Oh no! You did it twice!"

Later that day, when my childhood curiosity took over, I asked, "What's it like to have a baby?" Beads of sweat began forming on my mother's forehead. She got the book and showed me a smiling woman in a hospital bed with a baby in her arms.

"Where did that baby come from?"

Mom ever-so-slowly, with her hands now shaking, pointed to a picture of a woman giving birth which showed the opening from which the baby was coming and said, "From here."

"WHAT?!"

She calmed me down by feeding me chocolate chip cookies. This brought up another question. "What do babies eat?"

With her handkerchief, she blotted her soaking forehead, then showed me a picture of a baby sucking the mother's breast. "Mom, what exactly is going on here?"

"Milk comes out of the mother's breast."

"WHAT?!"

That evening I said, "I wish I was a boy. They don't have to do this sickening stuff."

Mom took a deep breath and said, "Babies can only come if there's a mother and a father. Your dad had to give something to me so that we could have you."

"What did he give you? Perfume? A doll house?"

"He gave me . . . seeds. With your father's seeds you grew inside me."

"Seeds? From where?"

She found a picture of the male anatomy and pointed. "From here."

"Oh my God, Mom! You haven't told anybody else you two did this, have you?"

She gently held my hands and said, "Every grown-up knows about this."

"WHAT?!"

"Saralee," she continued holding my hands. "My happiest times were when you and your brother were babies."

And so, the most important thing I learned from my mother, other than the milk and seed thing, is that there is nothing that matters more in life than the love we give.

Especially if it's in the form of chocolate.

Valentine's Day Hunk
By Lisa Tognola

Ladies, are you tired of the Valentine's Day "same old's?" Same old jewelry, same old candy, same old man? This Valentine's Day, bypass the tennis bracelet and the roses and forget the box of chocolates, because you can get all the delicious eye candy a girl could ask for when you join the **Hunk of the Month Club**!

You can never go wrong with **THE GIFT THAT KEEPS ON GIVING**.

We have a variety of trophy husbands ready, willing and able to serve as your personal ambassador of hotness, status and youth. That's right, trophy *husbands*. After all, why should men have all the fun?

Sound too good to be real? It is, but so what? Real is overrated. These fictional hunky husbands are made of medical grade plastic and are as close as you'll get to the real thing and still make good on your fantasy *and* your marriage. It's the ideal situation. You get to keep your marriage intact and have some fun on the side because these life-size hotties are designed to fulfill your every whim, and they come with a full head of hair!

Selection, Quality and Value are what set us apart from our competitors. Our standard model comes with a muscular physique, moveable arms and legs, and a head that will instantly swivel in your direction when you call his name. He is anatomically correct (although certain body parts may fall off when wet) and his underwear is permanently molded to his body so you won't have to pick it up off the floor each morning. For custom orders, you can choose the circumference of his neck, chest, waist and other unnamed body parts.

Each of our hunks meets rigorous quality control standards and is programmed to say all the right things (accents available in English, French and Italian):

"Yes, of course I'll be home for dinner."

"You relax, honey, I'll feed the dog and take out the garbage."

"Have you been eating enough? You look like you've lost weight."

Testimonials:

Tina, New Jersey: *I loved my March hunk, "Rough Around the Edges" Vince! He had an earring, slicked back hair, and was cut like a Hershey's bar under his muscle shirt. I can't wait to try "Jack hammer" John in April!*

Muffy, New York. *I was crazy for my December hunk, "Urban Sugar Daddy" Dan ---that mane of wavy brown hair, painted goatee, and chiseled cheekbones ...mmmm ...*

Katie, California: *September's "Suburban Rock Band" Spike had that sexy brooding thing going on. He had a fierce look, and wore a wicked grin that really turned me on. His "Mattel for grown-ups" tattoo was cool, too. I had fun dressing us up in matching leather accessories!*

Order Today!

Be a trendsetter and brag to your friends that you score a new hunk every month! Treat yourself to an original gift---a Valentine's Day Hunk. Remember, if you don't like him, you might like his best friend. . .

Hunk of the Month Club (3 Months) *See price sheet for extended rates and custom orders.

Today: $175.99
Compare at $~~189.85~~
You Save: 15%
Review: 5.0 *****

The Hunk of the Month Club: He's not your grandma's crash test dummy.

People who viewed this also viewed:

Adult Toys of the Month Club and Thong of the Month Club

Clothing and accessories sold separately, available while supplies last. Gift membership also includes free extra parts.

WARNING: This product is not recommended for people with pediophobia (those suffering an intense, irrational fear of mannequins).

Charlie decided to buy a special Valentine's Day gift for his new girlfriend, Ruth. They hadn't dated long, so to make sure the gift was right for her he took his sister shopping with him for a woman's opinion. She suggested a nice pair of gloves, which Charlie thought was perfect. While in the store, his sister bought a pair of panties...and the clerk mixed the two items up. He mailed his gift to Ruth, with this note:

Dearest Ruth

I chose this Valentine's Day gift as I noticed that you often don't wear any when we go out in the evenings. If it had not been for my sister, I would have chosen the ones with buttons, but she prefers short ones that are much easier to remove.

These are a lovely color. The lady at the store where I bought them showed me the pair she had been wearing for the past three weeks, and they were hardly soiled at all. I had her try yours on for me and they looked quite lovely. I wish I was there to put them on you for the first time; no doubt, other hands will come into contact with them before I have a chance to see you again. When you take them off, remember to blow on them lightly before putting them away as they will naturally be a little damp from wearing. Just think how many times I'll be kissing them in the future. I hope you'll wear them Friday night for me. Love, Charlie

The Valentine's Day Massackwards
By The Weekend Warrior (a.k.a. Linton Robinson)

Valentine's Day is, simply, Love Day. With the exception of your odd massacre, it's not about Valentine at all. Whoever he was. Some pussy-whipped Roman flit. It's all about Love. "Love" in the sense of "Having Somebody to Take You Out Somewhere Expensive and Give You Things."

Which would be a pretty simple transaction, except our entire concept of what Love means has gotten cluttered up with all those sayings people take as truth, leading to misunderstanding and the sort of homicides that misunderstandings justify. It"s time to examine some of these seemingly benign maxims and weed our facts from foibles.

For openers, it's widely stated that All's Fair In Love And War. Not so. Let's examine this one in specific detail:

1. Poison Gas: unfair in both, although perfume is generally excepted.
2. Lying about marital status: considered unfair in love, merely ineffective in war.

3. Surprise and sneak attacks: fair in both, though unsporting.

4. Biochemical tactics: unfair in war/ widely advertised in love. Because warfare operates on the Geneva Convention, as opposed to the more conventional conventions of Paris. Or even conventions of Shriners.

5. Taking no prisoners: frowned on in war, merely cost effective in love

6. Two-timing: unfair in love, OK in war, but difficult. The problems with wars on two fronts has been discussed, but not as widely as difficulties with the beast with two backs.

It should be obvious at this point that these homilies are not always what they seem. Let's just cast a cold eye on other saws, mots, and chestnuts that confuse our inevitably confused approach to the other sex.

• Love makes world go around . False. Love can make *your* world go wild. Or kablooey. But the rest of us will not be moved.

• Love don't last, cooking do. True. Where are preservatives when you need them?

• Love conquers all. False. Or there would be no soap operas. War doesn't conquer all either. That's the whole point. Half of it has to lose.

- Love is blue. False. This notion probably comes from "Blue Movies." Otherwise who knows what they were thinking? Actually, love is pink inside.

- All you need is love. False. It's like saying all you need is money. Or youth. Or looks. Or a ladder as tall as the well you fell into.

- Love means never having to say you're sorry. False. Actually, it's superior firepower that means never having to say you're sorry. You hear people in love saying how sorry they are all the time.

- Love hurts. True. But not as bad as the lack of it. When you look down a calendar of American holidays and commemorations, Thanksgiving and Love Day really jump out as the least crazy reasons to celebrate.

Valentine's Date
By V. Karen McMahon

I had a big date on Valentine's Day,
A very special date, you might say.
You see, I'd tried three times before,
And never made it to this gal's door.

Each date I made, a tragedy would occur,
And always stop me from getting to her.
She had warned me, enough is enough,
Don't show this time, and things will get rough.

I was so excited, what can happen this time?
The farm chores are done, things will be fine.
I knew I'd finally get to be with her now,
Then I remembered – I hadn't milked the cow!

So with my bucket in hand I rushed outside,
And that damned old cow kicked me in the side.
I lay on the ground unable to breathe,
No, no, not again, she'll never believe.

In pain I arose and got ready somehow,
Not even broken ribs can stop this date now.
I showed at her door and she let me inside.
She wouldn't see me wince—I had my pride!

As the night wore on she started to sense,
That something was wrong, I was stiff as a fence.
So I told her the story and it made her sad,
But touched that I'd come when feeling so bad.

But instead of the love I thought she would show,
She said, "That cow knows something I don't know.
Maybe I'm a gal you're not supposed to be near,
Something bad happens every time you are here."

So with a heavy heart I headed back home,
Doggone it, now I'll spend another night alone.
But wait, the cow's still here and this is her fate,
I might be alone, but I'll eat a good steak.

(For a friend that this really happened to, except the steak
part)

So, It's for Women?
By Leanne Morgan

They say men don't really care about Valentine's Day. It's for women. It's this women thing and you have to buy your wife and girlfriend nifty things on Valentine's Day because that's what they want.

So what do *men* want? They want a woman to do nasty, vulgar things to them.

So how do both people get what they want? Well, I heard this guy on television saying what we should do for our guy. He said, "You know, do a surprise. Dress up in something, like a nursing outfit. Or a French maid."

Lord, if I put on a French maid outfit, I know what Chuck would say. He'd say, "Leanne, fetch the 'Spick and Span.' We're going to fix these baseboards that you haven't washed the whole time we've been living here. I'm going to dust them, then you go over them with Spick and Span."

Then, just after I have ruined my back from a whole day of doing baseboards, *then* he'd come up to me and try to "mount" me, I guess is what people say. I'm sorry if that's nasty or anything. I don't mean to be. It's Biblical. I'm married.

Don't Surprise your Valentine
By John Philipp

You are a man. You have a woman in your life. You love her. Valentine's Day is coming up. You think, instead of the traditional gifts of flowers and candy, I will surprise her this year and buy her lingerie.

STOP!

In that one-sentence thought you have committed five deadly relationship sins. If you are a man reading this, sit down; this may get uncomfortable. If you are a woman reading this, stop snickering and get your man a cup of coffee. He's gonna need it.

Let's go back over your thinking process. *Instead of the traditional gifts of flowers and candy.* If you plan to depart from tradition, you better have a pretty compelling reason such as, "Oprah made me do it." Even if you give her a diamond-ruby studded bracelet, you are still expected to cough up flowers and candy. She will *notice what's missing* more than what's there. You don't want to start Valentine's Day with, "You didn't give me candy. Omigod, you think I'm fat!"

I'll surprise her. I know. You're thinking, when one makes an effort to surprise someone, it's greatly appreciated. That was true when you were seven, the age, apparently, at which your mental development slowed to a crawl.

Women do not like *surprise*; they like *expected*. They want to be able to count on you. Understand that everything you do will be reported to her local Sisterhood branch. "Jimmy was so cute on Valentine's Day. He bought a new chain saw and carved the old stump in the backyard into a heart." You're putting her in a corner when she has to justify your actions to other women. Cornered women attack.

And buy her lingerie. This simple statement actually masks a complex thought for a man, but you love her so you made the effort. You are thinking, "She wants to look sexy for me and who knows better what I find sexy?"

Men have logical brains, a fact on which they pride themselves. The more complex a problem is, the better. "The Giants are trailing the Pirates 3 to 1. It's the top of the sixth. One out, men on first and second. Randy Winn is at the plate; Barry Bonds is on deck. The Pirates shortstop is limping and the hot dog vendor just surfaced one section over with a full 40-pound 'hot box'. Should Winn bunt?" Men love these kinds of problems, ones that are complex, multi-faceted and contain sports and food in the same question.

This complex logic ability men are blessed with excludes situations involving women. If a man is having a two-part thought involving a woman, he's wrong on at least one. This is what has happened in your case.

She wants to look sexy for me is a true statement on the face of it but, as in most cases, truth has a subtext. The "you" she wants to look sexy for is not *Today You*. It is *Tomorrow You*. She sees you as the man you will become and, in fact, has devoted her life to seeing that you get there. Tomorrow You has very specific tastes as to what he thinks is sexy. She knows what they are. You don't because you haven't gotten there yet.

And who knows better what I find sexy? It's a legitimate question. We just answered it: *she* does.

If these arguments haven't convinced you, consider the following: *a lingerie store is no place for a man.*

- There are no other men there.

- There are pictures of partially clad models everywhere; this means you will be thinking with your Junior Brain.

- The store personnel will tell you that 75% of women are wearing the wrong size bra. They won't tell you that 74% of women deny that statement.

- You will have to touch the products. Touching a bra containing a live breast is one thing. Touching unfilled, delustered, floral tricot is quite another.

Consider this: to make a purchase you will, at some point, find yourself standing in the store, an item of scanty apparel in your hand, in front a pretty woman approximately the shape of your lady and saying these words: "Try this on."

You will be damned to hell for doing that.

Two Love Poems

A poem by woman
Before I lay me down to sleep,
I pray for a man, who's not a creep,
One who's handsome, smart and strong.
One who loves to listen long,
One who thinks before he speaks,
One who'll call, not wait for weeks.
I pray he's gainfully employed,
When I spend his cash, won't be annoyed.
Pulls out my chair and opens my door.
Massages my back and begs to do more.
Oh! Send me a man who'll make love to my mind,
Knows what to answer to 'how big is my behind?'
I pray that this man will love me to no end,
And always be my very best friend.

A poem by man
I pray for a deaf-mute gymnast nymphomaniac with
huge boobs who owns a bar on a golf course,
and loves to send me fishing and drinking. This
doesn't rhyme and I don't give a damn.

Because They Only Deserve the Best (Well, the Best Free Stuff)
By Lauren Stevens

It's February and naturally I feel obligated to write something about Valentine's Day. On the 14th I'll probably go with a piece about hot lovin' (oh yeah, you should check back for sure). But when we speak of the most sex-filled holiday of the year (not counting Secretary Appreciation day), I figure we should talk about gifts… the best kind of gifts… cheap, creative, last-minute gifts….

A true gift from the heart.

1. Nakedness. Really I could stop here. From what I've gathered over the years, guys love naked chicks. They'll settle for lingerie, but ultimately the more naked the girl, the more happy the man. So what to do while naked? Well anything. But here are a couple of ideas if you're stumped…

    *   Dance Naked: Sure stripper experience is best, but any old jig will do. Personally I think a friggin' naked Riverdance would work. My man says I'm wrong, so I might just have to put it to the test.

*Note: I apologize to those who know me for the visual (especially to you, Dad).

- Cook Naked: Cook him dinner in the nude and he'll be salivating for your buttery, steaming hot rump. *Note: For sanitary and safety reasons, an apron is okay for this. Getting burned from hot wax is one thing, burned from hot oil off the stove is a whole other.

- Ooh la la... a pasta dinner. Naked!

- Follow anything of these with Sex Naked and you've hit a home run for sure.

2. Make a Love List. God this sounds cheesy, but if your guy's got a sentimental side, he'll love it. Make a list of memories, moments and things you love about your man and your relationship together. It could be the way his eyes crinkle when he laughs, or when you had sex in the snow at Big Bear, or the time he tripped down the stairs at the family reunion. Make it a list of 10 things, or go crazy and make it 100. Either way read it out loud to him, relive the moments and then add another. Wink, wink.

3. Learn to Play the Harp / Compose a Love Song. Hmm... five days is not a lot of time for this. Perhaps best to wait until next year. Also note this may not be the gift for every man – it takes a special one to appreciate the sound of an angel.

4. Mystery Massage: Blindfold him and give him a massage he'll never forget. For added adventure, use different household items for unique effects (i.e. grill brush, duster, cat comb).

   - He loves that old brush already. Just imagine if you sexed it up!

5. Script a Sexy Story: Write a hot, seasonal story or poem and read it to him naked (remember the power of nakedness) or in a homemade Cupid costume – minus the diaper. Instead think red or white lace panties, thigh-highs and wings (make them with coat hangers and panty hose or buy some for under $10).

6. Bubble Bath: Sure it's kind of predictable, but you get a soothing bubble bath out of it. Add an extra splash with a game of clues to lead him from the front door to you in the tub. Everybody's bound to get wet with this gift (I'm talking about the water people, jeez)!

7. A Mix Tape: Super unique, old school, personalized gift. And since he'll never be able to find anywhere to play it, you don't actually have to record anything.

   - What a sweet, creative - albeit useless - gift honey!
   - It's the thought that counts, but he'll never, never know that's all it ever was.

8. Naughty Coupons: Like the Mix Tape, sexy coupons are great because they almost never actually get used! Just kidding(ish). Go ahead and print out promises for

a romp in the car, a marathon sex day or something new he's always hinted he wanted. Have fun with them, because if they DO get used, you'll want to enjoy it while he's cashing in. Maybe even include one for "A night in to watch Rocky IV or Transformers." What a lucky guy!

9. Homemade Sexy Pictures: Take them yourself (or have a good friend help you)

   • He'll think of you every time he sees the bed. Wait, he already does, doesn't he?

   • and present them to him one at a time throughout the day. Or let him take the pictures himself for his gift. Just make sure to retain control over which ones get deleted or not. Note: Use your best judgement here! Do not give these pictures to your man unless he is a mature adult who will not post them on Facebook, like a childish douchebag.

10. Lingerie: Okay this costs a little money, and it's not exactly nakedness, but you probably need a new bra anyway, right? Lingerie rocks as a gift because he'll love it, but you get to pick it out (and make sure your ass doesn't look too big/boobs too small) and you get to keep it. Or flip it and get your man some sexy, tight, teal briefs... and then laugh at him.

Happy Valentine's Day, Dear
Here's your Mesh Body Stocking
By Ernie Witham

Christmas is officially over. Today I dragged the tree with its fifteen remaining needles out to the curb, tied the Christmas lights into one great big ball like I found them, and dumped the odd remains of two ham-a-ramas and a jalapeño cheese log into the cat's dish, which caused him to immediately jump up onto the telephone stand and look up the address for the humane society's self-admittance wing.

But it's done. Kaput. Finé. The Yule tide has ebbed. And not a moment too soon, because now it's time for ...Valentine's Day.

Not to worry though, because this year I'm ready. Last February I was fooled by the pact my wife and I made that we weren't going to bother with Valentine's Day. What I thought she meant was that she didn't expect a gift. What she really meant was that only a chump would think it was okay not to get his wife—who was put on this earth for no greater reason than to serve her husband's every need, although said husband could count on serving certain needs himself until further notice—a gift.

And even though it was quite a bonding experience camping out in my backyard in February with my brother-in-law, who had wondered why everyone was buying flowers on Washington's birthday, I think I'd rather spend the rainy season inside this year.

So I grabbed the garbage bag full of Christmas cards and wrapping paper to drop off at the local landfill, and headed off to the Hallmark store--that magical place full of those beautiful poetic musings that women love. I settled on a card with a romantic, soft-focused photograph of a young couple laughing and hugging in a wooded glen, taken no doubt just seconds before they realized they were standing waist deep in poison oak.

Then I headed across the mall to the lingerie store. The place was mobbed with guys all holding intimate apparel, trying to picture their wives in them. One guy was holding his selection upside down wondering, I suspect, why the thing had snaps at the neck. I was about to explain when a sales lady approached wearing a button that said "All Our Bras Are Half Off." She looked frazzled. Her hair was mussed. Her make-up was smeared, and she had bags under her eyes.

"Let me guess," she said. "Gift for the wife?"

Before I could compliment her on such a quick assessment of the situation, she moved me to one side and yelled over my shoulder.

"Please don't mix the satin panties up with the silk ones."

Two guys, who were each holding a dozen pair of panties, smiled sheepishly, like they just got caught during a midnight raid at the female dorms.

"I hate Valentine's Day," she muttered. Then with a forced smile she asked: "So, what did you have in mind?"

"I dunno. Something sexy, I guess."

"Novel idea. What's her favorite color?"

"Hmm...brown?"

"Brown? Brown's her favorite color?"

"Green?"

"You don't know do you?"

"Well, our cat is gray and white and she likes him a lot," I thought briefly about the cat and wondered if he'd still be there when I got home. Meanwhile, the sales lady moved me to one side again.

"Sir. Sirrrr."

"A large bald man in a three-piece suit glanced up.

"It's Velcro," she said. "As you have no doubt observed, it will make that same sound over and over."

She shook her head, turned her attention back to me, and was about to speak, when a tall, thin guy approached us wearing a teddy over his T-shirt and boxer shorts.

"Whataya think?" he asked.

I thought the red was a little too bright for his complexion and was about to say so when the sales lady jumped up onto a clearance counter and addressed the entire store.

"Okay. Here's what we are going to do. I want everyone of you to take out the amount of money you want to spend and step up to the counter. I will hand you an item that costs that amount of money. Do not worry about the color or size. Your wives will be in here to exchange your gifts tomorrow. Now, who's first?"

We all hesitated. She held up her watch.

"The mall closes in fifteen minutes, gentlemen, and they are predicting a particularly cold February this year."
I thought I caught a whiff of damp tent. Then I quickly took out my wallet and got in line.

Love is the only game that is not called on account of darkness.
Thomas Carlyle

Love is the triumph of imagination over intelligence.
H.L.Mencken

Presents of Mine
By Dan Burt

My wife is still furious about Valentine's Day. Not because I forgot the holiday, a holiday that causes otherwise reasonable fellows to make last-minute dashes to the nearest gas station for the perfect present that says "I love you" (such as a NASCAR keychain fob or a dusty "Color Me Badd" cassette). No, my wife is irate because I bought her a present. Let me explain.

I have an affliction, a disorder, a handicap, a bane, a curse: I have trouble choosing presents. Oh, I've sought help--books, workshops, therapy--but nothing pans out. My therapist thought I was making progress and encouraged me to buy a Valentine's gift this year. I was apprehensive, but decided to give it a try even though my wife had not forgiven me for buying her a baseball cap with attached radio and a Hooters t-shirt for our anniversary.

I was nervous but began to relax as I performed my pre-shopping rituals that included deep breathing, meditation, and stretching. In thirty minutes, I was loose, limber, and lucid (the three L's of shopping). Later, I realized one of my mistakes (besides listening to my therapist) was shopping at a club store where everything is in bulk. But my love for my wife is a bulky love so I searched the warehouse until I found the one thing I knew would delight my beloved.

When I proudly gave my wife the present, she eyed me and the package with wary suspicion, like a judge staring at a repeat offender. After prodding her for several minutes, she eventually opened my gift of love. Intuitively, I sensed she was a bit disappointed.

"What the hell is wrong with you?!" she said as she heaved the ten-pound bag of frozen chicken wings at my head.

I'm not the only one in my family with the unpropitious gift-giving gene. My Uncle Roland was infamous for his ill-conceived offerings such as ceramic banjos and lavender boxing trunks with "The Assassin" emblazoned on the seat. However, his generosity came to an end at the last family reunion when several members of the family became ill after contracting E. coli from his gifted abstract mud sculptures.

Now, I fear I may have passed the unfortunate gene to my young son. The other day he presented my wife and I with some pathetic contraption he called a "boat." My wife told him it was the best boat she had ever seen. I was dumbfounded. I couldn't believe my wife would become enamored with my son's deformed boat (which I doubted would even float), and yet become enraged when I presented her with a heartfelt Valentine's bouquet of gift-wrapped chicken wings.

"That probably wouldn't even float," I said as I snatched the pitiful thing away from my startled son. I raced to the bathroom and dropped the boat in the toilet. Just as I suspected: it sank like a ceramic banjo.

"What the hell is wrong with you?!" my wife said as she hugged our crying son.

Don't be surprised if one day he needs therapy after giving his spouse a neon futon for Valentine's Day.

Valentine's Day is when a lot of married men are reminded what a poor shot Cupid really is.
Anonymous

Love is grand. Divorce is a hundred grand.
John Waters

Love is the magician that pulls man out of his own hat.
Ben Hecht

I'm with Cupid
By Joel Schwartzberg

What holiday is less connected to its historical roots than Valentine's Day? Jesus gets a strong shout-out here and there on his birthday. President's Day may be the perfect occasion for an underwear sale, but at least Washington's face graces the newspaper ads. Even Punxsutawney Phil got a movie deal. But where is St. Valentine? Weeks before February 14, local stores celebrate enthusiastically with cheap jewelry, heart-shaped placemats, heart-themed pajamas, and enough chocolate to keep dentists busy through 2020 – yet Valentine himself is treated more like Voldemort.

The poor guy can't even catch any controversy. Nobody appears on Bill O'Reilly's show decrying the "War on St. Valentine." While public schools wring their hands about Halloween and Christmas, cutting symmetrical hearts from folded red construction paper is as much an American classroom tradition as doodling on your notebook and picking your nose. It's even a-ok to decorate the walls with underage, semi-naked predators, armed to the gums with bows and sharp projectiles. (And you thought Miley Cyrus sent a bad message).

The wide-ranging themes of school punch-out valentine cards best illustrates the modern disconnect between Valentine's Day and anything even remotely romantic. At one Target store, I saw Spiderman valentines, Darth Vader-themed valentine chocolates, and military camouflage tattoo valentines. Apparently, nothing says "I love you" more than tattooing your sweetie's hand with a green army bazooka.

Some people even think Valentine's Day was manufactured by greedy card companies, much like "Buy a Card From a Greedy Card Company Day," which never really took off.

Many women see no coincidence in the fact that Valentine's Day occurs only weeks after Super Bowl Sunday. Their explanation: Payback. Most men know this as well, so the card industry supplies them with myriad variations on the theme: "Dear, I've been a pretty mediocre mate for many months now and ignored you completely while watching men tackle each other between beer commercials, so here's a pop-up card with two chimpanzees making out and my name scribbled underneath. Umm, can we have a 'date night' now?"

The needlessly-kept secret is that actual Valentine's Day lore is rich with sacrifice, generosity, and blind love. Think Braveheart meets When Harry Met Sally, minus fake accents and orgasms. The story goes something like this:

Around the year 270, Emperor Claudius II banned marriages because he decided single men made better soldiers than married men. (It's understandable because single men can use both their hands for fighting, whereas married men always need one hand free to hold the remote.)

Well, a third-century priest named Valentine thought that was pretty bogus, and started performing illegal marriages waaaaaaay before performing illegal marriages became all the rage. (Take that, San Francisco!)

Valentine, "friend of lovers," got tossed in the slammer for his trouble, but met a charming young blind woman (as is often the case with the newly-incarcerated). He miraculously healed her blindness, after which the girl immediately exclaimed, "Hey, I thought you said you looked like George Clooney!"

Unfazed, he wrote her a farewell message, signed: "from your Valentine." The phrase stuck with us forever. Not so everlasting was Val, who was executed on February 24, 270.

This paved the way to Patron Sainthood, and "Saint Valentine" became the inspiration for a February 14 Roman festival during which young Romans wrote affectionate greetings to girls they liked or simply wished to enslave. This went on for hundreds of years until "St. Hallmark of the Mall" appeared on the scene, charged a couple of bucks for foldable cardboard, and reduced every tender thought between romantic couples into trite rhyming couplets. The rest is history. For more details, check out VH-1's I Love the 270's!

In a typical parental mission to replace ignorance with embellished truth, I shared the story with my kids, making St. Valentine a Jedi Knight and the blind girl a beautiful princess. The loving couple didn't die, but retired to Florida where they spent their final days playing shuffleboard and testing Whitman's Samplers.

As for me, I'm inspired to spend V-Day doing what Val would have done: Simply spending quality, TV-free time with the one I love…and buying her some shiny things. Hey, I may be romantic, but I'm no idiot.

If all goes well, I may also bring sight to a couple of blind people just for the heck of it.

I got a Valentine's Day card from my girl. It said, 'Take my heart ! Take my arms! Take my lips!' Which is just like her. Keeping the best part for herself.

Robert Orben

Um's the Word

By Mike Gallagher

"Um," I said.

Somehow, perhaps in the primordial portion of my brain, I sensed this was a trick question. Back in prehistoric times, answering that type of question incorrectly would have meant death. Now it's even worse.

Luckily, a guy can't go wrong with "um." Is it a sound or a word? Is it a commitment or a question? Who knows! I only wish "um" had been on my multiple-choice tests in college because I would have selected it every time and never been wrong. The beauty of "um" is it makes you sound stupid so no one ever thinks it's an indication of serious thinking.

While saying "um," my mind slipped into another gear, another dimension really, as it picked apart the question. First of all, I had to determine if the question really was, "What do you want to do for Valentine's Day?" Was it a matter of what I wanted to do? Was this day on the level of my birthday, when my wishes are primary, or even Father's Day, when I kind of get what I want as long as it involves the kids? I quickly ruled out those possibilities.

Valentine's Day is about love, and love is about putting someone else's needs and desires above your own. If the question was, "Since you're such a selfish jerk, how do you want to spend this day so that it brings pleasure only to you?" I could have answered that comfortably. I've been waiting for someone to ask me that question all of my life. I have given it the type of deep thought I typically reserve for contemplating the strength of the Seattle Mariners' starting rotation.

Somehow between the rising "u" and the sliding "m," my mind deciphered that the question was, "Honey, now take your best guess. What is it that I would hope you would think that I would want to do on Valentine's Day? This answer will reflect how well you know me, and whether you ever listen to anything I say."

This is a much more difficult question.

To be honest, I had to drag out the "m" half of the word so long my lips began to tremble. I was also on the edge of the danger zone — the five-second "um" — where it would sound like I was meditating.

I realized I couldn't say something like, "Let's rent 'Sex in the City,' and eat chocolates." That would sound like an answer I arrived at by Googling "Things chicks like to do."

I would need to say something like, "Let's rent 'Laura,' the noir flick where the Dana Andrews character falls in love with the Gene Tierney character even though he thinks she is dead. That's how much I love you, babe, you don't even need a pulse."

You wouldn't even be able to write that on a card because the sentiment would be so heavy it would break the post office scale when you went to mail it. You'd need an Obama bailout to pay for the postage.

Would it be over the top? It's hard to say.

Also, "Laura" is one of my favorite films so it might look like I was just repackaging something I wanted to do to make it look like it was for her.

Then I had a thought, the kind of thought that shows what I'm capable of thinking of when I put my mind to it.

I said, "I don't know, honey. What do you want to do?"

Thinking of what the one you love wants, that there is the essence of Valentine's Day.

You can't put a price tag on love, but you can on all its accessories.

Chico Marx

If You Want Loyal and Devoted, Then Buy a Dog
By Suzy Soro

When I'm in a relationship and Valentine's Day looms I know it's make or break time. If I survive the day without using automatic weapons it could lead to marriage. If I don't make it and find myself explaining blood stains to the sheriff it could still lead to marriage because I truly have terrible taste in men.

I've had trouble with them from the moment I started dating. My first boyfriend got hit by a truck. My second boyfriend had a heart attack. My third boyfriend called me up one day and said, "You know something; I think you're a jinx." "Really, how do you figure?" But then the phone went dead because he was only allowed ten minute calls from prison.

I've been engaged three times and each one of them proposed on Valentine's Day. It was somehow fitting that I got engaged on a day where hearts are displayed with an arrow through them.

For the first wedding I bought a long white dress. For the second I bought a long off-white dress. The third time I just bought something I could return.

People always ask me why I never got married. When they do, I look up long enough from counting my stacks of money to laugh. Then I put on my diamonds and furs and ring for the butler and he call for the chauffeur and soon I'm in my Maybach heading for another fun day at the plastic surgeons. And I don't have to check with anybody and can spend my money however I want which does not include having to buy a new hot water heater and other things I can't wear.

I'm convinced this inability to land the plane occurs after many years of bad Valentine's Days. When you've received one too many cards written in iambic pentameter and signed, simply, "Bob." Not "Love, Bob" because that's a written commitment and there could be a court date in his future with a signed contract like that.

I take responsibility for all this failure because I always look for the wrong things in a relationship. Instead of compassion or kindness I look for a man who cooks, because I don't. I'll eat out, I'll take out, *I'll put out*. But I'm not cooking. When I get my dream house, I'm not even going to build a kitchen. I'm going to put a KFC in on the ground floor.

I salute anyone brave enough to weather the shark tank of love. My problem is that I'm not sure people can be faithful to each other. If only we took a page from the animal kingdom. For example, the bald eagle mates and remains faithful for life. Of course if he had some hair he'd probably be out screwing around.

The best thing about Valentine's Day is the valuable lessons we invariably end up repeating because we don't get them right the first time:

1. Relationships require sharing and compromise. (What kind of living hell is that?)

2. You're not supposed to go to bed mad. (I wasn't aware there was another way to go to bed)

3. Some people should have all their shopping privileges revoked for life. (And by "some people" I mean "men")

Thankfully these days I'm so busy I look forward to Valentine's Day. It's the only way I really get to spend time alone.

Love is just a chocolate substitute.
Melanie Clark

If love is the answer, could you rephrase the question?
Lily Tomlin

Why You're Single This Valentine's Day

You believe in fate

You own a beanbag chair

You are wearing Looney Tunes clothing

You are bald but you have a ponytail

When you eat dinners out, your orders come back to you in buckets

You know the lyrics to the "Thundercats" theme song

You've nicknamed your goiter

You stood in line at midnight for the new Harry Potter movie opening. You are 43

You are ugly

Your cell phone ring is a song from a former winner of "American Idol"

You wear cut off jean shorts in public

You wear cut off jean shorts, period

You do your grocery shopping with your pet Burmese python around your neck

You're unlovable

Inequity

"Happy Valentine's Day, sweetheart," I say. "I love you so much."

I hold a gift she's presented me in my hand. "You didn't have to get me anything," she says, holding the gift I gave her in her hand.

"I wanted to," I say. "Because I love you so much."

She opens the gift in her hand. "Oh my God," she says.

"This is beautiful."

It's a ring.

"Do you like it?"

"This is…" She's speechless.

"It's my great-grandmother's ring."

"…" She's still speechless.

"My great-grandmother was aboard the Lusitania. She was recently engaged. That was her engagement ring. She was coming back to the Old World to be reunited with her love again. She was in the States because she was in a theater group touring the East Coast. She played piano. She was the most wonderful piano player. She left New York to return home, excited, of course, to see her fiancé again. Even with the war on she knew the power of true love. The love I feel for you."

"…" She was speechless and listening to my great-grandmother's story.

"She was so close to being reunited with her love, you know? But the German u-boat attacked. Boom! The boat was torpedoed and sank in less than twenty minutes a few miles off the Old Head of Kinsale in Ireland. So sad…Sadder still because my great-grandmother wasn't one of the fortunate ones that made it onto one of the lifeboats. She was adrift on the ocean."

"…." She's speechless and crying now a little.

"When they found her, her hand was gripping this ring. She must have loved him so much. Her hand was gripping this ring and…" I get choked up a little. "…and, the worst part is that the day she died was her anniversary with her fiancé."

She's crying now, looking at the beautiful ring on her finger.

I'm crying now a little, too, but I shrug it off. "I just love you so much."

"…"

"What did you get me?" I ask.

I open the present. Inside is a giant Hershey kiss.

"…"

❤

161

Do Not Take Your Valentine's Day Date to the Following Locations:

Chuck E. Cheese's

Minor league baseball game

Niece's bassoon recital

Paintball World

Favorite strip club

Pixar movie

Grandfather's funeral

Ex-wife's best friend's BBQ

DMV

Sports bar

IKEA

The back of your van

Ways Not To Show to Your Doubtful Girlfriend That You Take St. Valentine's Day Seriously

You command people to beat you with clubs and, afterwards, behead you.

Some Valentine's Day Haiku for The Lonely

Oh, single again
Another Valentine's Day

Spring for a hooker

I do not need her!
I can do better than her!
Blow up doll returns

Prep: Frugal V-Day
Ten bucks for local hooker
Gratis clap: Priceless

Inappropriate Valentine's Day Gifts

Tickets to the ball game
Box of chocolates left over from Christmas
Vacuum Cleaner
Herpes

The Differences in Valentine's Day Coupon Books Given to Spouses

Him: Will wash the car, nude.
Her: Will run your children to karate lessons for the umpteenth time
Him: Will wash the dishes, nude.

Her: Will balance the checkbook. Please remind me again why we needed the new motorcycle?

Him: Will iron your clothes, nude.

Her: Will make you breakfast, lunch and dinner without complaint for the umpteenth time

Him: Will eat breakfast, lunch and/or dinner, nude.

Her: Will go grocery shopping again. For steak, you like flat iron, right?

Him: Will vacuum, nude.

Her: Will continue to work for the pharmaceutical company to try and make ends meet since your part-time job as a minor league hockey team mascot doesn't really bring in any much needed money.

Him: Will make sweet sweet love to you, nude.

Her: Will try and stay awake while you try to have sex with me for the umpteenth time.

I wanted to make it really special on Valentine's Day, so I tied my boyfriend up. And for three solid hours I watched whatever I wanted on TV."

Tracy Smith

A Letter to the President
RE: N.G.V.D.
By John Boston

"The most romantic thing a woman ever said to me was: 'Are you sure you're not a cop?'"

— *Larry Brown*

Dear President Obama:

For lo these many years now, I have been unsuccessfully lobbying for equality in America. As a male, I am confident that it has not escaped your attention of a crime being perpetrated against our gender by the alleged members of the fairer sex.

You know.

Women?

Let me cut to the chase.

We men feel you need to introduce legislation or at least appoint yet another czar to create (*blare of trumpets, switch to NFL Films Booth Announcer's Self-Indulgent Bass Voice*)

"NATIONAL GUYS' VALENTINE'S DAY!!"

N.G.V.D.

Gay. Straight. Single. Married. Anglo. Of color. Every February 14th, we fellows must endure the psychological and often even physical anguish of celebrating a holiday forced upon us by both big business and mushy women.

Or, as they like to be called in Politically Correct circles:

Persons of Mush.

And don't get me wrong, Mr. President.

Women have a right to their mushness and/or mushnacity.

P.O.M.s (Persons of Mush) have a right to enjoy their gender-biased Valentine's Day, with its flowered doilies and diabetic-coma inducing boxes of See's. There's no crime in their littering all flat surfaces with pink plastic flowers, uncountable Snoopys with stomach-wrenching cutey-isms or Teddy bears stuffed by Third World street urchins with lint, cat fur and recycled plastic bags and brandishing the greeting: "I Wub U."

Or, in Spanish: *"Te Amo-wub."*

It is the P.O.M.s' inalienable right to melt upon opening a bath set. Although the obvious implication in giving someone a gift like this is that they smell bad. And of course, we guys aren't at all inwardly smirking while an invisible thought balloon appears over our heads: "Oh great. Essence of Uber-Mart — Clean up on Aisle 46B, Please..."

Bless the girls' hearts, each and every one of them on this, the high holy day of Girl Romance.

But what about us guys on February 14th?

Barack — is it just me?

I don't think I'm the only guy in the civilized world who goes a-twitter upon seeing the buttcrack of a poorly drawn little cherub with wings and an archery set that would get him laughed out of Field & Stream Magazine.

Mr. President.

I'm a guy.

And I have a question:

"What in the H-E-First-Two-Letters-Of-Llama am I going to do with an ozone-depleting helium-filled, straight-to-the-landfill pink tin foil balloon with 'Wubby Dubby Hubby' boldly stenciled across?"

Barack.

I want a National Guys' Valentine's Day.

Let the women keep theirs.

You're in The White House.

Allegedly.

Word is, you have some pull in Washington.

It's in a rare cycle when the halls of both houses are populated with libertines, mooncalves, thick-ankled former hippies, guitar strummers, perverts, steely-eyed Tea Partyers and Democrats. Every day, on C-SPAN, I see some generic congressman stride to the podium to make a

Davy Crockett-like speech extolling the virtues of his district. Every three minutes, between Tuesday afternoon and Wednesday morning when Congress is in session, during every third month, bills are passed to honor everything from National Donkey Girl Scout Month to making Medical Marijuana the state plant of Vermont.

Mr. Obama. I'm asking. No. Pleading. Create the L.U.M.A. Act of 2011.

It stands for Leave Us Men Alone.

Pick a day.

August has nothing, virtually nothing happening in it. Pick a day in August.

No male in America has the courage to utter this.

But this is what we want from women:

Serenity.

No tasks.

No outings.

No decorations.

No reservations.

No painful lines at the lingerie shop where we have to answer the question: "Well what size is your wife?"

You rub the back of your neck with a sun burnt, calloused hand and start talking like Daniel Boone:

"Well. She'd be big. Real big. Couldn't quite make it through the Panama Canal. Her underwear was so huge, she has to wash them in sections. Why, a herd of bison could take a week to cross her heinie…" squint to look at the name tag, "…Alice."

We men don't want to spend our holiday with "Guy" in it installing air conditioners or being hollered at by N.G.s.

(Non-Guys.)

We don't want to waste our national 24 hours sitting on a red Naugahyde bench at Coco's with 389,684 sullen other guys accompanied by bored women all wearing the same expression: "I could have done better."

Say the magic word: LUMA.

Leave Us Men Alone.

Just let us wander out to the beach and fall spread-eagle on the sand for a day.

We know.

We'll get a sun burn.

Let us escape to the golf course and just not even finish the third hole. We could just take a nap under a tree.

Don't remind us of our single-digit IQs, our lack of sex drive, our sub-zero Sensitivity Factor, disinterest in our career, family, life or waistline. Let us sit on a curb somewhere, eating ribs, sucking the barbecue sauce right out of the plastic container and throwing the bones to our new friend, the feral dog.

Let us fall asleep — in LUMA fashion, butt saluting the ceiling — as a compendium of Super Bowl Moments on ESPN2 drones on at volume 2.

Make it a law, Mr. President, with strict penalties if broken (and no opting out, like in You-Know-Whocare).

Give us men a day — maybe in August — with no social obligations or feigning interest with out-of-context smiles.

For the love all that is true, holy and unspoken in America, let us men rest.

Please?

Our Amazing Humorists

(A.K.A. The Usual Suspects)

Michael Andreoni decided, after several decades of being referred to as a sarcastic nit, to revel in it. He lives near Ann Arbor, Michigan. Michael's stories and essays have appeared **in Pif, Iconoclast, Fogged Clarity, TQR, Hippocampus**, and other publications. Michael's very short story "Wednesday Morning Rodeo" was nominated for the **Pushcart Prize** in 2010, and can be read online **at Thumbnail Magazine**.

Amy Bagwell has dreamed of being a writer since last night. In her day job, she uses her many skills and talents as a cook, maid, nanny, therapist, chauffeur, social director, event planner, administrative assistant, procurement manager, and whore. Her turn-ons are going to the gym, pinot noir, and baking cakes. Her turn-offs are flatulence, interrupted sleep, and rejection letters. Amy contributes to the **Greenville, South Carolina, News**, a senior resource magazine, and several small journals. Her creative non-fiction can be found on her blog, **www.puffofinspiration.blogspot.com**.

Barb Best won the 2010 **Erma Bombeck Global Humor Award** for her essay on sex and sleep at **Humorwriters.org**. Her work has appeared in **The New York Times, The L.A. Times, Saturday Evening Post**, and **Today Magazine** among others, and performed by prominent comediennes, including Joan Rivers. Read her at **Divinecaroline.com** and **More.com**, in addition to her own blog **www.barbsblast.wordpress.com**. Follow Barb on Twitter: @HaBarb.

John Boston is one of America's top humorists and political satirists: winner of over 119 awards across the country, culminating in the **Will Rogers Lifetime Achievement Award**. His adventure/comedy novel, "**Naked Came the Sasquatch**," was required reading at Harvard. He lives on Scared o' Bears Ranch in Santa Clarita, California, with his 8-year-old daughter, Indiana. Fans of Johns voluminous past work are certain to enjoy his new venue, **TheJohnBostonMagazine.com**, His latest novels include the Orwellian, "**Adam Henry**" and the much anticipated/dreaded "**Honey, I Never Slept With Sarah Palin**."

Dan Burt is an ardent bibliophile, but don't say so out loud because he suspects it is illegal in his home state of Alabama, where he currently lives underground with his wife and two sons. Not only is Dan imbued with fancy book learnin' junk, he's also quite experienced in the way of the world. Dan is the creator of the humor website Captain Canard**, www.CaptainCanard.com**. You can follow him on Twitter @danburt**.**

Joan Oliver Emmer is a market researcher, budding social worker, blogger and Trophy Wife. She hopes one day to develop a comedy routine invoking all four identities, in the form of a monologue or, more, likely, a Greek tragedy accompanied by an off-key chorus. She is also mother to two boys, who go by the code names Thing 1 and Thing 2 to protect their identities (obviously). Read more about Joan and her life living large in New Jersey at, not surprisingly, **www.JoanOliverEmmer.com.**

Robert Ferrell is author of well over two books. He also has won awards as a calligrapher and fine artist, bookbinder, iconographer, photographer, woodworker, and semi-finalist at the **2011 Robert Benchley Society Humor Writing** award. He is a classically-trained percussionist and performs with many musical ensembles, including the folk-rock group **Restless Wind**. His books, variously described as "brainy fiction," "bitingly clever social satire," and "File Not Found," are "**Tangent**" and "**Infinite Loop**," the tongue-in-cheek fantasy novel "**Goblinopolis**," the award-winning hallucinogenic novella "**Infinity or Bust**," all on amazon.com and/or Scribd.com.

Patty Friedmann has always lived, aside from slight interruptions for education and natural disasters, in New Orleans. She is technically married until she gets Medicare. She is the mother of Esme Roberson and Werner Friedmann II and the crazed grandmother of Summer Roberson, Kennedy Friedmann, and Carmine Friedmann. Patty has been a prolific and celebrated writer with many inclusions and accolades. Her two latest books are a YA novel, **Taken Away**–finalist for Small Press Book of the Year in 2011– and a literary e-novel, **Too Jewish**. And of course a humor book: **Too Smart to Be Rich**. To see those titles, and her half-dozen darkly comic literary novels set in New Orleans, check out her website, **www.pattyfriedmann.com** and **author page** at amazon.com.

Eve Gaal got a miniature typewriter for her fourth birthday, and her life was never the same. Following writing for college newspapers, she launched a career including restaurant columns for a Newport Beach, California, newspaper, newsletters for the world's third largest amusement park, and using her God-given talent to influence unwary consumers to want new cars. Eve's work is published in the "**God Makes Lemonade**" anthology, "**Fiction Noir**" from Hen House Press, and "**Goose River Poetry Anthology**." More of her writing can be found on her blog, **www.thedesertrocks.blogspot.com**.

Mike Gallagher writes a weekly humor column for the **Daily Record**, a daily newspaper in the small college town of Ellensburg, Washington. He has written his column for the past 25 years and has received state, regional and national recognition. He has been nominated for a Pulitzer Prize for distinguished commentary 12 times, an honor not diminished at all by the fact he has nominated himself each of those times. Gallagher's influences include but are not limited to Art Buchwald, William F. Buckley, Jorge Luis Borges, the Marx Brothers and his mother. Read more at **www.dailyrecordnews.com**

Sarah Garb is a collector of intercepted love notes and a distributor of Loud Pills before performances. She offers the opportunity to read eight-year-olds' tips for how to have a successful marriage or the most recent thing that elementary school kids think is really cool (spoiler alert – it's most likely going to be Fake-Picking One's Nose.) All those wonders can be found on Sarah's blog, **www.sarahgarb.blogspot.com**. Her writing has also appeared on **McSweeney's Internet Tendency**, in **Mountain Man Dance Moves: The McSweeney's Book of Lists**, and at **An Army of Ermas.**

Kate Heidel is a humor writer and one-time Jersey Girl who steered clear of any Real Housewives of Jersey Shore by moving to Minneapolis. She has been writing her funny/scary humor for years, notably her regular columns in the presumably satiric **Happy Woman Magazine, CAP News**, the aptly named **Postcards from the Pug Bus**, and has had her work translated into French for the arty French send-up of Vogue-like mags**, Nunuche**. Ground Zero for Kate's post-edgy humor is her site, **www.wearyourcape.com,** which since 2009 has partnered with **HumorFeed**, a provider of daily humor and news satire.

Cammy May Hunnicutt isn't really particularly funny. First and foremost a Southern Belle (though currently at large) she is also a total bitch. Or so her admirers say. Recently retired after half a lifetime in the modeling trenches, she has been writing and editing screenplays and completing her first novel, about a tough female investigator whose enemies resemble her various boyfriends. It's not funny, either.

Mark Hunter is an emergency dispatcher and volunteer firefighter in Albion, Indiana. He lives with his fiancée and a cowardly ball python named Lucius, and has two daughters as well as twin grandsons when he isn't chasing sirens and crises. His column **"Slightly Off the Mark"** has been carried in northeast Indiana newspapers for twenty years. Mark's first novel, the romantic comedy "Storm Chaser" was released by **Whiskey Creek Press** in 2011 and a collection of related short stories, "**Storm Chaser Shorts**" will appear in May of 2012.

Leigh Anne Jasheway is a humor writer, comedian, and stress management expert. She is the 2003 winner of the **National Erma Bombeck Humor Writing Award** for her true story on how her first mammogram caught on fire. She teaches at both the University of Oregon and Lane Community College, runs a comedy troupe, is a humor columnist for the **Register Guard's Dash Magazine**, and is the former host of "**Women Under the Influence of Laughter**," on KOPT 1600 AM. See Leigh Anne's seventeen books, including "**Bedtime Stories for Dogs**," "**The Stressed-Out Woman's Guide to Letting Go with Laughter**," "**Don't Get Mad, Get Funny**," "**Not Guilty by Reason of Menopause**," and "**How'd All These Ping Pong Balls Get In My Bag!?**" at her website: **www.accidentalcomic.com**.

Blythe Jewell is based in Austin, Texas, from whence she sallies to use her humor talents for good—though sometimes in a kind of evil way. She is known to thousands for her blog **www.themusicalfruit.net** as well as her sporadic attacks **on Funny, Not Slutty, BlogHer.com**, and as part of the national **Listen To Your Mother** event. Her most recent projects are a collection of poetry, "**Stupid Poems About Random Everyday Things,**" and a dark comedy novel too devastatingly brilliant to name here.

El Kartun is a *nombre de plu*ma much better known in Mexico than his given name, Jesus Pedroza. Though a fine artist and instructor on the side, El Kartun is Tijuana's most dominant cartoonist. The dean of strolling caricaturists, he also draws the only regular local comic strip for the daily "**El Sol de Tijuana**". His book, "**Despertad**" is a unique and innovative melange of graphic novel, comic, and literature.

Henry Lefler is a sixth grader who has enjoyed drawing since he was in kindergarten. He particularly likes to illustrate and explore life's many challenges through the art of cartooning. In his spare time, he also enjoys playing piano, boxing and putting his dirty clothes in the hamper. (That last bit is not entirely true.) Henry is single and lives in Santa Monica, California with his family, including his mother, who wants to be just like him when she grows up. Henry prefers drawing and "performance art" to publication at this point in his career, but his mom, Anna-- author **of The CHICKtionary**-- writes mild aftertaste humor at **www.annalefler.com**.

V. Karen McMahon was born and raised in southwestern Virginia, but has lived many years in the state's "horse country". Her career included owning and managing an art and gift shop. After many years working as an editor and writer for several companies, culminating in consulting work after retirement, she decided to turn her writing skills to personal writing. To date, she has authored books, short stories, poems and song lyrics. Karen's recent work includes the thriller "**Back There**" and "**I Saw A White Horse Today**", a children's book that fits well with her environment. She has a collection of ebooks as well. See more of her work on her personal website: **Writings By Karen**

E. Mitchell is an award-winning humorist, novelist, playwright-ist with literary bling from **Thurber House**, the **Robert Benchley Society** and the **Will Rogers Writers' Workshop**. Anthologies include **Chicken Soup** and **A Cup of Comfort** as well as non-brothy books like "**Bad Austen**," and "**In the Peanut Gallery with Mystery Science Theater 3000**." E. (e. for short) is author of the sci-fi humor novel "**The Amazing, Incredible Shrinking Colossal Bikini-Crazed Creature from the Public Domain**," recently adapted for the stage in San Diego and Chicago, heading for Broadway via the Donner Pass. The **2010 Writer's Digest screenwriting awardee** currently dishes the **Film Hound** blog for the **Seattle Post-Intelligencer**. Seek further befuddlement at **www.emitchellhumor.com**.

Leanne Morgan is unusual even among stand-up comediennes: a mother of three from an Appalachian farm whose comedic blend of southern charm and hook'em story-telling has brought her to national broadcasting, film roles, books and CD's and a sitcom in development. A moonlight job selling jewelry at parties led local bookings, then Vegas competitions and spots on "The View". Her website at **www.leannemorgan.com** lists her tour dates, as well as videos of her "**Thou Shalt Laugh**" tour with Sinbad and "**Happiness Is**" with Willie Nelson, the Dalai Lama, and John Cougar Mellencamp. And, her hilarious solo CD, "**You'd Be Crazy, Too**."

Michael Mulhern was Boston born and bred, but found that a Boston College degree and career wasn't for him so he wrote a book. Found out that was hard too. When love, Canadian-style came his way he braved the paperwork to follow her to Canada, but ended up in Vermont, working at the Von Trapp lodge in Stowe, which means he essentially owes his job to Julie Andrews and a few catchy tunes. This period of adjustment has led to some weird writing, which can be sampled at **www.helium.com/users/267966/show_articles**

Jason Offutt lives in Northwest Missouri where he teaches college journalism, and uses his superpowers for good. His books include, "**Paranormal Missouri**," "**What Lurks Beyond**," "**Darkness Walks: Shadow People Among us**," "**Haunted Missouri**," and the collection of humor essays, "**On Being Dad**." Jason's newest book, "**Paranormal Missouri: Show Me Your Monsters**," is available for order from Amazon.com. You can find more of Jason's work at his blog, **www. from-the-shadows.blogspot.com.**

Jackie Papandrew has written for many humor anthologies, including the **Chicken Soup for the Soul** series, and newspapers such as **The Cleveland Plain Dealer**, **The Tampa Tribune** and **The Oklahoman**. Her honors include a **Neal Award** from American Business Media and awards from the Oklahoma Press Association, Parenting Publications of America**, America's Funniest Humor Press** and the Florida Freelance Writers Association. Jackie's books, including "**The Desperate Dad's Guide to Getting Some**" and "**Airing My Dirty Laundry**" are available, along with other sources of mirth, at her website, **www.jackiepapandrew.com**.

Barry Parham writes humorous columns, essays and short stories. Music fanatic, 1981 graduate of the University of Georgia, and self-described eco-narcissist, Barry won several awards for the stories, "**Going Green, Seeing Red**" and "**Driving Miss Conception**," in his 2009 sleeper, "**Why I Hate Straws**." To find out why he hates straws, and experience his other humorous collections, "**Sorry, We Can't Use Funny**," and the Politically Incorrigible "**Blush: Politics and Other Unnatural Acts,**" as well as follow his columns and appearances, see Barry's author page on **amazon.com**.

Saralee Perel is a longtime lover of Cape Cod, and her humor column, after running for years in the Cape Cod

Times, is now syndicated in over 40 papers nationwide. A frequent contributor to **Chicken Soup**, **Family Circle**, **Woman's World**, **Pet Gazette**, **OCEAN'S**, and many other national publication, she is also an essayest for the **Christopher and Dana Reeve Foundation**. Her column regularly receives top awards from several press associations. Her novel "**Raw Nerves**", A Cape Cod comedic thriller, was selected for **Booksense** by the **American Booksellers Association** and is available on amazon.com.

John Philipp writes a weekly humor column for five Marin County newspapers. John has won numerous awards including the **Mona Schreiber Prize** for Humorous Fiction and Nonfiction, the Grand Prize in the Fall 2007 **Contest for** *Memoir (and)* magazine, and was awarded second-place by the National Society of Newspaper Columnists for the best Humor Column in 2010 for newspapers under 50,000 circulation. His humor may be read under johnphilipphumor at gather.com. Thought~Bytes may be viewed at http://thoughtbytes.gather.com/. His book of wise/witty sayings, "**Rolph's Thought~Bytes**", was illustrated by Phil Frank: his novel is "**Perfect Parts**."

Gregg Podolski struck early. At the age of nine his story "**Buck, The Horse Raised By Wolves**," a cautionary tale about capitalism's growing influence on the global socio-economic landscape (with horsies) ran in **Highlights Magazine** after a brief legal dispute over foreign subsidiary rights. Since then, Gregg's humor columns have appeared in **The Philadelphia Inquirer** and **Philadelphia Daily News**., though he chooses to live in New Jersey with his wife and daughter. His first novel— **"ANDROIDS, NINJAS, FLOSS: A MEMOIR (BUT NOT REALLY)"**--is being prepared for publication even as you read this.

Tim Rickard is one of the funniest guys alive. Not usually said about Mensa Members who graduated from Kentucky Wesleyan. In addition to his multi-awarded comic strip **"Brewster Rockit: Space Guy"**–syndicated by **Tribune Media** and a hilarious warping of SF settings and icons to his own fiendish satires–Tim has illustrated three dozen book covers and drawn for publications ranging from **Better Homes** to **The Washington Post**. Follow Tim's comic strip adventures of the starship R.U. Sirius, his blog at the **Greensboro, N.C. News and Record**…and definitely check his probably dangerously funny book, **"Brewster Rockit: Space Guy, Close Encounters of the Worst Kind"** on amazon.com.

Dorothy Rosby is a speaker and humorist whose column has appeared in newspapers in ten Midwestern and Western states since 1996. (The area is home to more cows than people, so the reader should not be overly impressed.) A former radio announcer, she was once asked by an employer to change her on-air name because "No one will take you seriously with a name like Dorothy." All of this has led to self-esteem issues that can only be dealt with by a healthy dose of self-deprecating humor. A two-time winner of the **South Dakota Press**

Women's Communications Contest/Humor Column category and second place winner in the **2010 National Federation of Press Women Communications** contest, Dorothy also writes for **Exceptional People Magazine** and **Black Hills Woman** magazine. Learn more at her website at **www.dorothyrosby.com**.

Joel Schwartzberg is Media Director of a **PBS** newsmag, former head writer at **Nickelodeon**, founder of the **TIME For Kids** website, and contributor to **The New York Times Magazine, Newsweek, The New York Daily News,** and **Chicken Soup**, as well as winner of too many awards to even think about. Yet primarily thinks of himself as a father, public speaking champ, and **Wheel of Fortune** fail. Joel's website at **www.joelschwartzberg.net** is inspirational, as his most recent, award-spangled book, "**The 40-Year-Old Version.**"

Lorraine Sears has finally managed to successfully disguise herself as a responsible adult, but she's a writer at heart. Her work has appeared in e-zines, magazines and anthologies; you can even buy a few of her short stories for your e-reader, published and sold by **Untreed Reads**, among them some notable titles are "**Big Red,**" "**Pumkin Lie,**" and "**Wasting Time,**" which are also available to buy through the likes of Amazon Kindle and Barnes and Noble. She is married, living in Buckinghamshire, UK with her husband, two children and assorted pets. Lorraine edits the **Red Asylum** ezine (**www.theredasylum.webs.com**) and **Writers Beat**

Quarterly while sounding off at **www.red-lorry.blogspot**.com and **Helium**

Jim Shea was born in Connecticut, where he has lived all his life with the exception of college and "two unfortunate weeks in law school". He is a full-time humor columnist **at The Hartford Courant**, where he writes about pop culture, baby boomers and politics, and does television commentary. He is also the author of two books: "**Too Shea**," which is a collection of his columns, and "**Huskymania**," which recounted the University of Connecticut's rise in men's and women's basketball.

Jonathan Shipley is a freelance writer living in Seattle with his wonderful daughter. His play, "**Deviled Eggs**," a humorous look at his painful romantic life, was produced and performed at the Blue Heron Theatre. His poetry has been published in a German welding magazine. Seriously. It was romantic poetry for welders. He is currently at work on a novel about cubicle life and finding words in the dictionary that'll make his daughter giggle. Jonathan's prolific work is widely published, including the **Los Angeles Times, the Boston Globe, Diner Journal, Fine Books Magazine, Lexus Magazine,** and **the Boston Globe**. Not to mention **Hobart Pulp, Seattle Salmon, Yankee Potroast** and **Cap'n Wacky**. Other anthologies include "**Mountain Man Dance Moves**," and "**The McSweeney's Joke Book of Book Jokes**." He edited the book "**Bat Boy Exposed**" for the **Weekly World News**. More on this amazing, weirdo, writer can be experienced at **www.jonathanshipley.blogspot.com**.

Suzy Soro is familiar to many from her appearances on TV shows like **Seinfeld** or **Curb Your Enthusiasm** or over fifteen standup comedy shows including **Comic Strip Live**, **Caroline's Comedy Hour, Starsearch,** and **An Evening at the Improv**. Suzy has toured with both the U.S.O. and M.W.R. and toured Germany, Holland, Macedonia, Serbia, Korea, Johnston Atoll and Japan. She also produced and toured with her own standup group, **Single, Married & Divorced**, for eight years. Suzy blogs **www.wherehotcomestodie.com.** Follow her on Twitter at @hotcomestodie.

Lauren Stevens is an Executive Producer, Showrunner, and Writer in the TV and film industry, with credits at **VH1, MTV, ABC, ESPN, Comedy Central**, and **Spike**. More recently, she produced digital programming for **Sony PlayStation** and **Mattel**. She has recently turned to novels and humor writing. See Lauren's humor and observations on her website at **www.laurenastevens.com** and her blog with the cheerful name.

Karla Telega is a humor writer with a particular eye to the baby boomer generation. She is a graduate of the University of Washington, the class of too long ago to remember. She co-founded and edited **The Laughing Trapezezine**, a monthly humor anthology, and is a regular contributor on the nationally syndicated **Skirt Magazine**. Karla's articles have won two awards in the National Humorpress writing contest. You can read her humor blog at **www.telegatales.com** or enjoy her funny mystery "**Box of Rocks**" at **amazon.com** or **adorobooks.com**.

Lisa Tognola is a Jersey Girl, where daily life as a suburban mom is fraught with challenges and unexpected dangers like adult dinner groups, town hall meetings and home shopping parties. Rather than fight fate, her outer mom embraced it by unleashing her inner columnist, reflecting weekly on life in the burbs—the good, the bad, and the ugly. Lisa's column at **The Alternative Press** is called "**Main Street Musings**," but her own blog is, **www.mainstreetmusingsblog.com**. Her work can also be seen at online magazine **More.com**. Lisa is also a contributor to **Funny Times Newspaper** where her parody of Oreo cookies was recently featured alongside humor greats Dave Barry and Garrison Keillor–an experience she found so stimulating, she had an **Oreogasm**. On twitter: @lisatognola.

Rachel Turner started blogging after the birth of her son in order to be the first to let the world know that, as a new mom, she had no idea what she was doing. She kept blogging because people were begging her to (and by people she means her mother). Born and raised in Atlanta, Georgia, Rachel has taken mystery writing on the road for twelve years. Her "**Make It A Mystery**" party business requires that she carry a crime scene in her car at all times. In addition to writing and hosting private and corporate mystery events, she has written two full-length dinner theater mysteries, "**This Song is For You Mr. Hitler**," and "**A Christmas Carol**" competition, which were performed across state lines in federal jurisdiction. Rachel blogs at **www.rachelshumor.com**.

Dawn Weber is a Buckeye lifer who graduated from Springfield Local High School in 1987 then went on to get a bachelor's degree from Kent State University, where she majored in flammable, piece-of-shit cars and cheap beer. She currently resides in Brownsville (Motto: Indoor Plumbing Optional) with the husband, kids and an ever-changing series of dirty, ill-mannered pets. Her resume includes work at newspapers, corporations and state government, but she's resentful about that. Her goals include thinner thighs, a nap, maybe a solo trip to Walmart. Dawn's humor has been delighting readers of her "**Lighten Up!**" column in the **Buckeye Lake Beacon**, which has won awards that don't seem to impress anybody, even her. It's well worth following her **www.lightenupweber.blogspot.com**, blog unless you are a faint-at-heart wuss.

The Weekend Warrior is a *nom du mud*, an imaginary playmate, a figment of a sick imagination based on the title of a cult classic column once syndicated in dozens of weekly papers that should have known better. While purportedly a guide to weekend behavior–mis or otherwise–it became obvious early on that the **Weekend Warrior Column** was actually a very unwholesome bit of verbal ledgermain, if not actually subversive. This seems to have increased its popularity, a sad commentary on our times. Worse yet, it's now a *novel*, saints help us. **"The**

Way of the Weekend Warrior" is available, until saner heads prevail, at www.adorobooks.com.

Ernie Witham is a humor lifer. A contributor to a dozen of the **Chicken Soup** anthologies, he also syndicates his column from the **Montecito, California Journal** on the Senior Wire News Network. Best-selling side-splitter Christopher Moore has called Ernie "the Dave Barry of the West." In addition to his on-going, award-winning humor workshops, Ernie is a photographer, graduate of Brooks Institute. Admirers of Ernie's fine wit will want to check out page at **www.erniesworld.com** and his books, **"Ernie's World"** and **"A Day In The Life of a 'Working' Writer**."

CPSIA information can be obtained at www.ICGtesting.com
Printed in the USA
LVOW011151150112

263897LV00001B/1/P